Portable Homes

Filled with parts and pieces

collected

by Lexie Bean

inside art by Laura Grothaus

outside art by Shelby Ziesing, Tails Williams, Thomas
Anyel Irving, and Steven James Ploe

To the women of my roots, who share my curved toes, oval eyes, and have lived in homes that looked like mine.

Love to,

The survivors that live these letters fully.

Mom and Colette and family: for knowing and trying and giving and for not knowing and not knowing what to give

Amanda/Kristin/Tails/Leah/Chris-Arora/Michelle/Calum/Korri: these beautiful people for their myspace pictures of blue hair and playgrounds, for overcoming their fear of my hairy legs, for dancing little dances with me in the crowded high school hallways, for building a family since the age of 9

Heather, Yoshimi, Lexi, Sarah, Meredith, Caroline, Davíd, and the writers of *Attention: People With Body Parts*: for making this thing living and breathing just by putting in pieces of themselves

Daniel, Ellen, Lisa, Ann, and the Oberlin Contact Improv Communities: who let me push back and love the bruises on my hips; who remind me that I am allowed to touch, like the elements, like a partner, like the glow of a wooden floor

Katie/Robin/Laura/Caroline/Zettie/Sarah/Shauna/Shosh/Rosie/ Hilary/Adah/Lena/Shelby/Val: the ladies and queer deers that make me feel stretched, inside-out, so so full; I imagine their insides filled with tinfoil stars

Gerard, Wes, David(t), Max, and Sam: boys who make music and poems that feel important; they rewrite everything I have been taught about men

Emily and Ilona: strangers that make me feel safe and close in a way that would make a great movie about the summer of 2013

And Jake Burns: who I could never leave out in a book about survival

Portable Homes

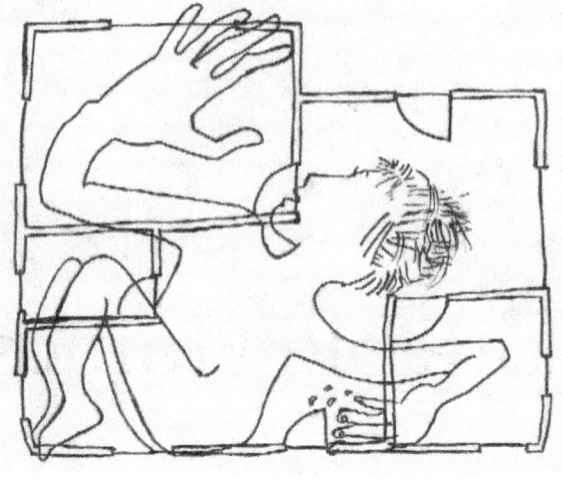

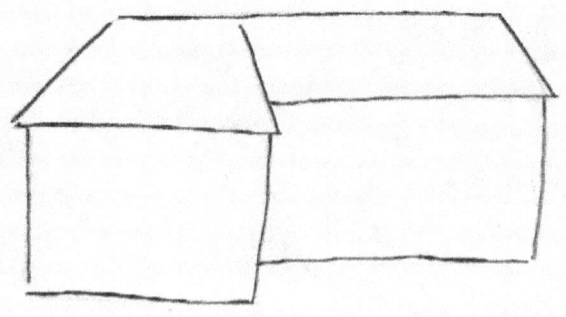

An introduction to building a Home

This carries letters written from domestic violence survivors who wrote their body parts. We write to reclaim, to heal, to build homes from the parts and pieces that are ours.

Do not be afraid to put this book down.
Do not be afraid to pick this book up.

This book is not heavy, but a release for those who have survived.

My small body crept down the narrow hall
Following a path my feet branded into the plush carpet fibers
As I called a name:
    It was a name that I heard rumors of at Girl Scouts
    A name that covered an entire wall in the Hallmark in June

Five years old,
I only know the name "dad" implied protection.

The figure waiting in the big room
    With the big bed
    And the big television
    Did not look like the fathers at the "Daddy Daughter Dance"

She moved awkwardly in a suit
She used a thick brown barrette to contain her wavy black hair
When she felt stressed

I called her mommy when I needed someone strong
I called her daddy when I needed something beautiful

These words carried my history, but at the time
They seemed like Magic

The word "mother"
The word "father"
Within one person
    Took root in a language I could not yet
Speak.

I was looking for love
Which is not always magic
Sometimes I could find it at the end of a narrow hall
Sometimes I could find it in the big room
    With the big bed
    And the big television.

At the dinner table,
I sat across the image of a father replacement eating fettuccine alfredo,
his favorite.

This man did not have my overbite
His teeth were slightly crooked
    And collected way more cavities than I ever could

However
He was my tooth fairy
He placed quarters under my pillow
    Every time my body shed evidence
    Of him.

I carried another man's overbite in my mouth
His long lose limbs under my clothes
And his blood in my chest

I started to look more and more like him as the years passed
Yet life happened.
Birthdays happened.
Visits from the tooth fairy happened.
Another marriage happened.

In a new home
    of broken chairs and bed springs
    and breath that smells like peanut m&ms
I felt uprooted
When I wanted to grow
    into my finger nails and sweaty palms
    and unshaven knees and split ends.

The Family Room
My fingernails

I never grew out my fingernails. I felt repulsed by the idea of
All the things I touched creeping into the cracks.

You're grounded:
I was told that girls in high school must have long nails;
They have fingertips that carve into scratched backs.
16th birthday and grounded for having nails and a body
    that defined their own growth.

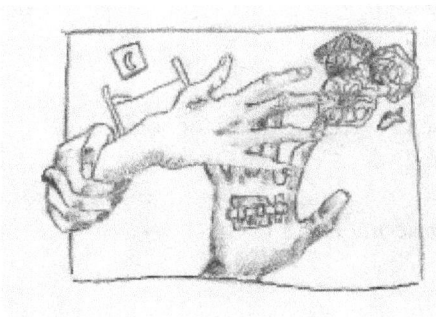

The Bedroom
My hands

It is June 18, 1998. My daily prayer:
Dear God,
I hope I have a good day tomorrow.
I hope he is in a good mood.
I hope they will think I am good.

I kept these thoughts latched between my palms.
I felt grateful for the sound of the ocean on days I forgot to put a
hamper in front of the door.
I wanted so badly to be good; to make good things with my hands;
and smile a good smile like the girls that sleep the whole night
through.

I looked to my hands when I wanted an escape to a place with a cool
breeze
And coral reefs strung together around my wrists
And a place I liked to call home.

The Bathroom
My knees

There is a light that peeks through the crevice of the bathroom door.
I turn on the faucet
And melt into the floor as I watch
   the motion and the murmurs in someone else's home.

Years deep into an eating disorder
My knees were my favorite body part.
They tip-toed, they touched, they kissed the floor
   Whenever I just wanted to see the light
   Of what cracked into the hurt.
My knees carried and moved all of the parts of me
That I had yet to grow into.

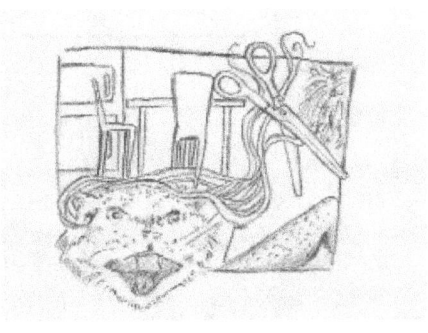

The Kitchen
My Hair

Your hair is mine
Why can you pet the cat, but I can't pet your hair
I paid for it--
I can touch it
Only pretty girls have long hair
Only sexy women have long hair
You are slowly turning into a boy
Faggot,
Hold still
Let me touch your legs

My hair;
it's mine. I moved away and cut it all off.
Held it in my hands and felt powerful.
Held another girl's hand and felt like
    I can be as much of a pretty girl or a sexy woman
    as my legs and hair and leg hair want to be.
This is to the time I refuse to hold still.

Attention:

These letters are to the times we refuse to hold still.
These letters are to the times the movement of our pores, belly, cheeks
   Gave us something to come home to
   When our homes were not something to come home to.

They map survival
As they carry the stories survivors lived in fully
   And grew into
   And carry away with a wholeness of a body that is ours.
These pieces are our homes.

Carry them with our hands full, fingernails laced;
Carry them away with legs that no longer care to tip-toe.
   They are yours to keep, share, and construct
   a body that is yours.

My hair; it's mine.

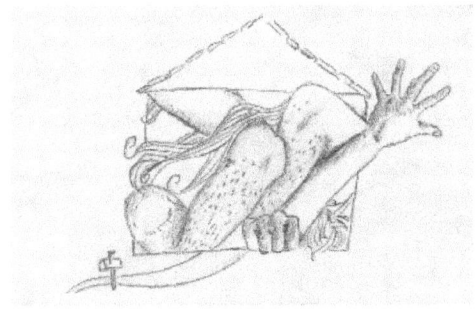

Contributors

This book holds one to three parts and pieces from the following people, listed in random order:

Karmilla Pillay-Siokos, Ashlyn Lincoln, Colleen Fusetti, Angie Ng, Amber Galey, Mitch Alexander, Alldara, Gregg Tyler Milligan, Tiffini Johnson, Lexie Bean, Betty Jean, Andrea Van Winkle, Doris M. Jones, Hilary Powers, LRB, Harmony Lyn, Kye Campbell-Fox, Shonna L Franks, Melissa Yearian, M. Osborn, Tails Williams, Athena Siokos, Marylyn L. Tesconi, A.D. Hogan, Katherine DiBiase, Theresa Mary-Clare, Laurie, Gwen, Leia, Sarah Doucet, Lolly Jayne, Ramona Riecke

Four writers wish to remain anonymous.

Layers

There are layers and layers of a lifetime of pain.
The layers are so deep that it's been hard to stay sane.
I have buried so much of my trauma.
I didn't want to show all of the drama.

Some of the layers have been pulled back.
Peeling them back has helped me get on track.
I try not to dwell on the past.
Because I know the shadows it casts.

Some of these layers I can't get rid of.
But I will keep trying with a little more love.
There are many layers of guilt and shame.
I'm trying not to make myself to blame.

All of these layers are pretty thick.
Fighting through them is the trick.
I continue to actively heal.
There is a lot of pain I still feel.

Many years of layers are seen on my face.
It's time for them to go they take up to much space.

Dear Head and Heart,

I know you are town different parts of me-but you are so connected like one. You both are on opposite ends of my body and both interact and react differently but you both are what makes me tick. I need you, head; to keep straight and heart; I need you to keep beating.

Head; when I was violated, I need you to know that you are strong. Even though we don't sleep very well and we relive the brutality of the rape on a daily basis-we are still here. That night, as much as we thought we were going to die, we didn't. Our body got bruises that faded eventually-but you and I kept thinking...living. We were left to deal...and we did and still are dealing.

Heart; you were so completely broken. Someone we loved so much fucked everything up. You and head were so confused. I'm sorry heart. I did not listen to you, I listened to head. In such a horrible violated thing that we went thru-I listened to head, which was smart. Not loving like you-you couldn't handle it. I know head couldn't either and needed help along the way-but I was really protecting you. Maybe one day you will feel again, but right now, you are on vacation because I don't want you to hurt again.

Heart; keep talking to head. Give head advice-but don't overwhelm. I'm sorry I cannot use you right now but one day I will.

Right now, head is important. If head does not work properly-you won't work properly. There is nothing the three of us can do to change the fact that someone we were so in love with could use and abuse us as much as he did-let alone hurt capsule we walk down the street in everyday.

I know he really fucked us up-but we are now free from it. Heart; you need to stop feeling for him. Quit telling head your love for him because he can never be with us ever again. Head, please know the difference of what heart keeps reminding you of and your thoughts and memories. What he did to all of us-that's not love. We need to move on and find someone that will allow you and heart to get along and be on the same page.

You guys need to get along-for my sake. One day I know all of us will get along, we just need to know how to work together. We will not give up on each other-we will keep working to make ourselves better. Take your time...I will be here waiting. Take your time. I just want you both to know-we will make it. We have come this far-thru a rape, a mistrial, a trial, a verdict, a calling off a planned wedding, watching someone we once were so in love with go to prison-self destruction-sadness-depression. We are still here. We are strong and we need to keep going. Lets do it for us. Lets make an example of a fighter-a strong woman. Live and let live. We can do it. It is still going to take time, but we are more than half way there. Push is all the way.

Love,
Me

Letter to (in) My Mind

My Dearest Mind,

Thank you for always being there for me. Today, I am turning to you both in thanks and in need. This letter will be difficult to write and I will jump back and forth, I know I will. But you will understand, as you always do.

I need to journey backward in time for healing that will be painful. And so, after asking my heart to envelope me and hold me steady, I turn to you, because I need you. I trust you finally to guide me and to gently release the memories that are so painful I don't even stay mindfully connected to them. But they surface from time to time, nagging and persistent. Sigh- you already know this.

So there you are- I admit it- I need you and I give thanks for you, for you are the keeper of the secrets. I deny their magnitude, I misread their intent, even as I fragment and disconnect and blame external factors. I do need you to help to make me whole.

Hold my hand- please?

As I begin to write this particular passage, it is early on a Saturday morning. It's a beautiful day and so very quiet in my house. The sun is shining, the wind chimes tinkle softly outside my open windows. I breathe in the summer air finally not fraught with humidity but a gentle breeze. The dogs lay at my feet, protecting me. This is the time I love.

The silence and the quiet. No noise, no television, no music even.
Silence envelops me – and this silence is warm and welcoming. It feels invited and I am grateful for it. We partner now this silence and I. We are finally friends, enjoying one another's company. Glad that the time that I would have interrupted it is now long gone. I know this is present and right now and not forever, so I bathe in you and find comfort in your presence.

My mind allows this now.

I give thanks and find time to reflect. I am not afraid to go backward in time. I will hesitate yes; I will suck in my breath and hold it until I am reminded I am doing so. But **I will do it**, I will go backward and inward into my brain toward the wounds that still bleed from time to time, and remind myself, I have the power to heal these wounds, my memories, those memories that you stored for me. I can only do so with you at my side.

I finally trust you now as I much as I trust my heart. So let's travel back. In all the time I spent with you, I never realized you were the one who kept me alive and sometimes in the dark, sheltered and comforted, safe from harm in your split second decisions to make me move, jump, deflect or simply retreat inside of you when the fear of "the voices" began. I didn't even really know what that was then- I simply reacted to your neurons firing, never understanding that you were protecting me even as I hid and chose to grow up protecting my heart from hurt, while you protected my body and ultimately, my tender soul.

Yes, so very long would it take to integrate the pieces of me.

You took me behind the couch to hide, or made me flee upstairs, or out into the yard, shielding me somewhat from noise. The noise I didn't even recognize as violence then. Isn't it funny how that carries on to this day? I will always put something in between me and another when I don't feel safe.

If I have to stand exposed and speak to others, I will hang on to a podium. If the situation is more personal, I will fold my arms or hold a book. When I lie down alone, I immediately cover myself with my blanket- but I put one foot out, always, always hoping to defy my own fear and hopefully stay connected to the world- always hoping to be a warrior and survive it all.

I was unconscious to all of it because you held it for me.

Oblivious was I, to the acts I engaged in to escape to some world of safety. The fantasies I created in my head. I decided that running away would be more perfect. Dreams of packing up my parcels and my baby brother and hopping the freight train that ran close by our house. Imagining it taking us both far away.

Even then you decided that the most tender part of me would first reach to help another. It's been a long time learning that this is not a weakness but a gift as long as I balance it with loving me first.

Yes, I would be the warrior, the savior; it was the only role I could play. The only way I could feel in control when the violence began. Lack of safety begets such terror for a child. One has to control it or simply feel out of control all of the time.

Even now, I will be usually go inside of you and write abstractedly and not in the first person when recalling events, to remove the pain a bit I suppose, to hold back.

But you Mind, are helping me change that- so the real events can be recalled, because really when the alcohol induced rage of my father had my parents fighting yet again, I fled inside of you. I owe you so very much.

Hold my hand while I remember, wont' you?

I remember one of the worst moments that you held for me. We were sleeping on the third floor, I must have been only five or six and for some reason, I was asleep in bed with Mom and a younger brother when the noise began. I still don't recall it all- just enough to be afraid and angry- but not to show it. At least not then. Another night of drunken rage.

It always began simply enough- singing and happy drunk bouncing up the stairs waking everyone who crossed his path. Mom would be annoyed and ignore him momentarily. Then not, and so it would begin. Angry words, loud voices, loud and louder. Deeper and more menacing. Trapped- inside the physical realms of time and space, I would lie there and pretend not to hear, cuddle closer to my baby brother.

Sometimes, the noise would stop- but not this night. On this night, the violence would reach epic proportions and I would finally run inside of you for safety.

A cigarette is lit in response to an admonishment not to smoke in bed lest you fall asleep.

"Don't tell me what to do."

I hear it in his voice. I hold my breath and tense. I am so afraid of impending doom- fire. Then another thought occurs to me. She is calm, my mother. Yelling, chastising, but I don't hear fear. What is that, what does that mean? Why isn't she angry?

Confusion.

Even at my young age I know this is wrong and we should be protected. Why isn't she doing that?

And then it happens. Her refusal to participate fully in his dance of anger sends him over the edge and the threats begin. The match gets struck, I smell the sulfur, I burrow further inside the covers as well as my mind. He throws the first one on the floor and it fizzles out. No reaction from the bed. A second one gets lit, and she reacts, admonishing him.

"Stop it"!

He grins. He turns to the bed, holding the pack of matches in his hand, and lights another one - and throws it directly on to the bed where we are lying. Another one, again and again and now I am screaming, I am racing around on the bed and trying desperately to put the matches out. Scurrying, like a small terrified animal, not even protecting my hands, just trying put out the embers and save us.

She is really yelling now and finally, reacting. Scurrying us downstairs to safety, waking the others on the way down to the living room, but still not out the door (lest the neighbors know), and so Mind/Brain, can you tell me the secret as of yet still locked inside of you and I?
What the hell took her so long? Why did I have to save everyone first? I was just a baby myself.

Even as we recall this together, I momentarily get angry again. Sometimes, I am madder at her than him. She was supposed to protect us first- not react to his madness first. Safety first, children first, the madness of their twisted relationship second. She had the order all wrong.

In the days that follow, I hear his words of apology, her pleas to stop drinking, his words stating she overreacted, he would never really hurt us. God help me neither of them understood the damage they did. Later, much later, when I would be old enough to understand what it was- I would stay inside my head and beg God to make them get divorced. To somehow take me away from this life of madness.

I made silent promises to both of us that no man would ever treat me that way- ever. I didn't realize then that you were protecting me, not the other way around.

So I know you will keep holding my hand, right?

I would be angry at her for being weak. And only now, as I write this, do I realize why I felt distanced from her emotionally, and totally removed from him until later in life when he exposed his sadness and weakness and pain. But back then, I would unknowingly begin to build an arsenal of strength and protection. I would put a shield around my heart and wield a sword of sarcastic wit with my words.

I would eventually leave them all- at the tender age of 16, I would run away to the first relationship that made me feel loved- and begin my disappearing act- the one that I would engage in with men for the rest of my life....-until you helped me learn.

Until you began to gently prod me and bring the memories back to me- you, my mind, the keeper of secrets and healing in juxtaposition to the reality of life as we presently know it and the safety that is necessary in the overall process.

The other memories that I still can only access in part, not in full, I now understand that you are holding for me. They will be released when the time is right.

I give thanks to you, Mind and Teacher, I recognize your power now- your abilities, your power to make me whole, for you are the safety net, the vault as well as the learned teacher.

You have taught me how to remember with healing, not pain, how to be vulnerable but safe, how to remember that the path chosen was not always easy, but we chose the family we were born to. They were human beings with feelings and failures and hurts of their own.

You Mind, gave me a gift as they each passed away, I was anguished for the mortal loss but more than that, I was …finally, liberated. You allowed me to understand that.

I understood that, as they were leaving me to travel the rest of my journey alone but not lonely. You taught me forgiveness is truly the greatest treasure and relief. You taught me that in death, if not in life, they are leading me and holding my hand and spurring me on greatness. They are now my teachers, providing me with the love, wisdom, safety and learning they could not give me when they were alive.

And I accept it- with love and with gratitude, that was only finally learned, and allowed, by you.

Thanks for holding my hand.

Dear Smile,

It's been awhile since I've seen you. Usually it's a frequent flyer. I see it in the morning when I look in the mirror starting my day. I see it during the day when your friend picks up on your contagious laugh to relieve stress or to make someone's day better. I see it at dinner time when we help little brother with homework and listen to his day. You are people's outlet when they are having a bad day and need to see a familiar face. Nobody likes to see you upside down. I've had many people ask questions about where it went. They know that substitute "smile" isn't real; they know it's just a show. I demand it's time to make a comeback. You have been gone way too long and that's one day too long. I know the days are tough, and some are long. Sometimes we can't fight back those tears, but some days we can. And those days we can are the days you are the strongest. You are putting yourself back together, like a puzzle. Your friends and family have been by your side. It's time to come back now, everyone missed you.

I hope to see you in the morning.

Love,

Beautiful You.

Dear Lady Parts;

I hope you are ok. I hope we are ok. I'm sorry that they hurt us, that they stuck their hands inside of us. I'm sorry that they touched us the way they did, that one stuck his penis inside of us. I have been trying to take care of us. I have made us off limits to anyone who might be interested in us. That's just to keep us safe.

Someday I want us to know true pleasure. I know I pleasure us from time to time. That's the only way we can feel safe enough to feel pleasure. I don't want us just to be used as a sex toy. I want us to know what true passion is.

I'm sorry I let you down. I'm trying to do better for us. Someday soon I want us to find someone who will treat us gently, lovingly, passionately. Not violently like we are used to being treated. I know that what happened to us wasn't our fault. So I just want you to know that we can feel loved and pleasure someday. I want us to be touched by another woman. I can never let a man touch us or enter us again. It would be like we are being hurt all over again. I won't let that happen. I will protect us with every thing I have.

Sincerely,
Yours Truly

To my Fallopian Tubes,

Once upon a time, many moons ago, you were fertile. Out of anger, I picked out a birthday present that harmed you. A surgery was performed that burned your bridge to V. No more eggs were allowed to travel nature's path. Where have they gone instead?

Do they now wander around until they give up all hope of finding a future? Do they begin an endless labyrinth to nothingness? Do they die amidst strangers who know nothing of their purpose? Do they feel as lost as I do?

I'm sorry that my rage ended your function prematurely. I had no good reason to play God. Five years after the procedure I felt your screams. There should have been another connection; another child. I cried with you and felt the weight of my decision. I missed the gift you wanted to give me.

In truth, I was afraid of your gifts. How was I suppose to keep them safe when I wasn't kept safe? What nation could I flee to? There is no safe place to protect these presents; not for forever. They grow and go away, they rarely stay, they are not suppose to.

Each of you, each tube, takes turns releasing a repurposed egg into my system. Before the journey onward, they prepare my focus with a mournful moan in lament for the broken, burned bridge before them. Silent sound reverberates outward to the end of each nerve prodding me to pay attention.

One by one, a new destination and a new destiny is discovered. Your eggs; our girls, have become acting ambassadors to each of my organs. What may seem like mayhem and madness is in reality magnanimous movement toward the best me I can be.

My digestive system no longer accepts refined gluten products full of preservatives. Our girls are no longer allowing fake things to pacify a hunger and need for the real meal deal. Eventually my over crowded jaw will stretch out more fully to accept the proper nutrition I now crave. Three molars from the back have disintegrated to move out of the way so that the remaining teeth can get use to having more room to function.

I thank you for your continued churning, keeping me on track each new moon. I also thank you for the recycled dreams each of our girls use to repair yet another part of me.

Dear Belly-Button,

At seven years old, I was convinced that you were the breathing hole for my future baby. I was too afraid to cover you, afraid to hide my future baby's mouth—afraid that she would feel stuck like my wrists under the blue sheets on that night our stepfather uncovered you.

I wanted you to be able to breathe, to spit out the words that his wet tongue whispered into you like a wishing well. To spit out the bones, the tongue, the cheek; your story is anything but tongue and cheek. You are real; you tether me to four generations of women whose wishes echoed into someone else's mouth. You remind me of my future baby: the one that knows that his words, his hurt, are not a secret.

Breathe slowly; I will never cover your mouth. My lifelines and un-brushed hair, my beautiful wrists and crisscrossed toes have all heard the news through your wavering breath.

But you survived.

Breathe slowly,
Stay with me
With love,

Dear You,

Hey, it's been a long time since we've spoken, since the last cortisone shot I believe. I just wanted to tell you, I'm still here, not in the greatest shape, but still here. Look, we need to talk about the Aleve and the everyday pain. I know, I know, I wasn't in the best shape even in high school, but there's something different this time.

I was wondering, and I know this is a touchy subject for you, was it from his hand? You know, the one that held onto me, dug in a little while he told you that you liked it? Does it still hurt like that when you crumble in the bottom of the shower on your bad days, and sob, even after 5 years? When I hurt, does it make you forget other pain? But Aleve everyday? You're gonna end up eating your stomach lining away; I know the shots aren't fun either.

I can't turn back the clock and I won't wish that I could make it all go away. I know you're strong enough to do this, I mean, you've been putting up with me since High School, so I know you're strong. The other body parts say the 8 times you actually did him before that night, were ok. But just that night, everything was off, nearly a year of being together too. Nose said it could smell the booze too. The Hips said they protected the newly discovered life in you, Heart and Brain will endure further, for however long you need to heal.

I'm sorry I can't be a better knee for you, but if we work together, we can make everything better. I miss that true smile, I miss the mile and a half jogs every night, I miss you good belly laugh. I can count on one tendon how many times I've heard it this year. Be good to everyone else too, will you? We all need you and you need us.

With love,

Your Left Knee
(I have Patellar Femoral Stress Syndrome, also known as runner's knee or "being knock kneed" on my left knee. It started buckling in in my sophomore year of high school. I'm 28 years old this year. I was raped the night I found out I was pregnant, by the same man who impregnated me, we had been in a relationship since March of 2007. I remember how much my left knee hurt because of how he held it. I

35

don't remember much else. I was admitted to the ER in March of 2012 for a breakdown, it was only then did I tell anyone about what happened late November 2007 and got some counseling. From this, I am a fully single mother, so I don't get as much help as I need; and I won't talk to my family because they aren't ready to listen yet. I've tried, I've even been victim blamed at one try.)

Dear Breasts,

I know this gets old. I know you've heard this a million times. But this is different this time. Its hard to explain. You know that I wish you were bigger. Fuller. See, right now, when I look in the mirror, all I see is a little girl. I know breasts don't make the woman, but it would help a whole lot if you would fill in a bit more.

When I see you in the mirror, I see myself through my father's eyes. I see his corruption. I see his attraction to his little girl. I don't see a 31 year old woman. I don't see a wife. I don't see a mother of 2 children. I see a young girl unable to deny her father's perversion. I think if you were fuller then that vision would end. I wouldn't see an underdeveloped girl, stunted by her father's abuse, dwarfed by incest. I'd see a woman.

To see myself as a woman would be a relief. A breath of fresh air! I'd be reborn, renewed! Free of the memories of him on my skin. Maybe I'd even be able to shake the permanent scars he left on my soul.

Do you think you could swell just a bit more? I'm not being greedy, I don't want to be huge by any means. I don't want freak show big, just bigger than what I have now. Enough to convince myself I'm a woman when I have to see myself naked. Enough to break the chains that keep me trapped in time. Just enough that I will stop reliving those nightmares from my childhood. Please?

Respectfully Requesting,

Dear Luxurious Locks that adorn my head,

Your chestnut coloring suits me perfectly. In the winter you darken, blending in with the cool air, matching my chocolate eyes. In the summer you become like honey, brightly catching the sun and reflecting its warmth. There's no need for any salon color treatments; your natural coloring can't be bought in any bottle. I love the way you cascade past my shoulders. You hide the scars on my shoulders while offering a teasing view of my phoenix tattoo. I know I get frustrated sometimes when deciding on how to wear you--up in a ponytail, in a braid, pigtails when I'm feeling playful, but usually leaving you down has the most dramatic effect. I wish I knew more ways to play with you! You're too long and heavy for most buns. And I never learned how to do the intricate braids.

There are times though... that I hold resentment towards you. I'll stare at you in the mirror and feel betrayed by you. Its not fair, I know. Its not your fault I grew you so long, long enough for my mother to grab and yank and pull out when she was angry with me. Its not your fault that she used you as a way to hurt me. I know this. But I can't help it, sometimes I just want to shave you all off. I get angry with how she would command control over you. I was envious of Billie Jean, from the movie The Legend of Billie Jean. I was envious of how she was able to commit to taking back control of her body by chopping off her beautiful locks of hair, creating for herself a new powerful identity. I couldn't do that when I was trapped by my mother's rule. She would've hurt me severely if I ever cut you. It would've taken the control away from her.

That resentment is silly. You didn't reach out to her. You didn't wrap yourself around her hands. You would weep when you lost strands to her grip. I know you felt guilt over the control she held over you. Sometimes I think you and I would be reborn and refreshed if I just chopped you up to my ears. I look at some women who have short hair and I admire them. I wonder if they came from abusive homes, abusive husbands or boyfriends, or lived with someone who destroyed them by grabbing their hair to gain a hold over the rest of their body. I wonder those things and imagine the relief they felt when they took back their lives by chopping off just one of the defining factors of their abuse. What courage they have!

Does that make me weak, keeping you so long? I don't think so. I wonder now if keeping you long is a way to stand up to my mother. She abused you, she took power over you, but I love you and care for you. I won't let anyone command you like she did. I'm not a little child anymore, subject to her demands and violence. I'm a woman now, in control over my own life. I look at you sometimes and feel triumph. I survived those awful days, and you're my trophy! I'll make you a promise, ok? I promise to only cut you when I WANT to, not when I feel feeble and scared. Because I am not afraid of my mother anymore, she has no power over me.

With Deepest Love,

To my amazing feet,

After more than a decade of being beaten, smacked across the face, publicly humiliated and told by the evil stepmother that:

Nobody will believe you.
Stop looking so sour.
You **think** you are so hot.
You have no figure.
You **need** my protection.
You are so stupid.
It is **your** fault.
You have no confidence.
You couldn't do anything with my help.
You are useless.

We were told something similar while in a dysfunctional relationship as a uni student.

Both times, we didn't walk away, because while we dreamed of freedom, we believed what they were saying.

Then through lots of work, we realized **they** were **wrong**. With courage, we ran as far as we could, dragging the burden of emotional trauma with us. While, we saw the world, learned many things and met lots of inspirational people, we we also met sexual predators, who added to that heavy load we were already pulling. However, it became easier to walk away from these people.

So now, dear feet, we are running around as an activist and academic, travelling the world

Thanks to you, my wonderful feet, for taking me far when others had told us that, without them, we couldn't go anywhere.

(untitled.)

the first time i told her i didn't like these lumps on my chest, she promised me she loved them. kissing, caressing, she breathed prayers into them and called me holy. i, she said, was her birth on venus, her statuesque goddess. i, once again, faced my own impossibility in the mirror of religion.

three months later, she held me down, this time with clenched fists instead of prayers reminding me how she loved the woman in me, the supple curvy waist and thighs, these doughy lumps on my chest. the pressure felt like nothing, a forced folding into myself.

she said i only disliked my lumps because of the misogynistic, racist queer culture that glorified white transmasculinity, testosterone, binders, and fundraisers for top surgeries.

the next week, she promised to love me back into acceptance with my body. she kissed and licked my breasts, buried curses or prayers deep into my breastplate. i can no longer distinguish holy utterances.

i learned a trick: pressure.
by applying pressure to myself, i molded my body into a shape i liked. i could reclaim the balled fists, the hands on my chest and body, the mouth that whispered into lumps of nothing. this daily act of pressure, now a ritual, is holy. i step into my binder, folding myself back into this body, resulting in sore ribs and weird posture. this chest - the recipient of 11 sir's, 3 ma'ams, 4 "i'm sorry's", and a lot of averted eyes on public transportation today - disrupts and soothes.

i don't let those sirs - hard fought for and never quite won - fool me; i don't escape misogyny or the violence of my past. my history - the night she knocked me down and flushed my anti-depressants down the drain in a dramatic sweep of apologies and refusals; the mornings she refused to let me leave her house; the control... now, my chest and i are who she never allowed us to be: self-determined.

two days ago, my friend sent me a poem. the poet stated, "there are ways of being a man that do not involve being a white man." there are ways of being masculine that do not involve racism, misogyny, violence, heavy/boisterous space-taking. the irony of masculinity being the refuge of violence and misogyny beats behind my breastplate, a strange phoenix refusing to be ignored wanting to destroy itself. i am reminded with each beat of a thousand old prayers spoken to my chest's strange existence and now blessed absence.

--

she had one thing right: the flesh stretched over my heart is holy. as i touch this skin today, i feel and hear beating, rhythmic life, controlled and articulated, organic and renewing.

i feel my chest rise slowly - barely tangible, each exhale a sigh of gratitude. my breath these days is short and shallow, no sudden gasps. i am no longer surprised when i feel that i cannot breath; white masculinity greedily fights for space in my lungs, under my bones. not even my soul has a free pass from white supremacy.

chest, may we beat and breath to a then-and-there one failure at a time, speaking and breathing holiness and forgiveness to all that you are. we are not yet whole.

Dear Right Forearm,

It's been over two years. I don't want to blame myself for how you were hurt anymore.

I trusted her with you (us) at first. She seemed very safe. Everything is always okay until it isn't. We met in our dorm and soon I was sleeping in her room every night. She always wanted to be the big spoon; she would cradle both you and my other forearm and curl the length of her body against my back. To be protected was okay until it wasn't.

She didn't want my body anyplace she couldn't monitor it. If I spent too long at the library or in the gym, she got angry. She said cruel things about my male friends and threatened to beat up a boy she thought had a crush on me. When I wanted to spend the night in my own room, she cried, because she said she couldn't sleep alone. I spent months trying to talk myself into leaving her and though I felt powerless, I could exert power over you. I starved almost all your flesh away and I gouged crescents into what was left with my fingernails and teeth.

I told her things were over on a Friday afternoon a few weeks before the semester ended. But I couldn't leave her, not as neatly as I wanted to. Can two people really be broken up if they still brush elbows while brushing their teeth? She came to my room to talk almost every night, seeking closure. Sometimes she would kiss me because she said she knew she could. Once she threw a wooden chair to emphasize a point and it grazed you on its way to tearing a hole in the dorm wall. You were injured, but it was literally only a scratch, a patch of peeled skin that hurt less than the tension I carried in my shoulders. I thought I was okay and that you were okay and that we would all be okay, because she bought me post-breakup flowers and shed fat remorseful tears.

I hoped I could be friends with her.

I tried to be friends with her like this:

I got stoned and watched cartoons with her and two mutual friends who weren't taking sides. She was staring at you and me like she was hungry. The drugs didn't dull the fear that thrummed through you every time she looked at me but we were going to be friends, weren't we? When we were walking back to the dorm, she asked me to come up to her room to talk. "Okay," I said, "but I'm too high to make any decisions right now."

(I don't know if I said that because it was true or because I knew what she wanted.) In her room you lay tensed in my lap as she told me how angry she was and how easy I was to forget. Her voice was raised and my head hurt, so I started to walk towards the door. She grabbed you and jerked me back and smashed her mouth on mine so hard that I could feel her teeth, even though my lips were closed.

She would not stop pressing into me. At first I tried to squirm away, but even after I went limp, she gripped you so tight and I felt like I was watching her bruise you from outside my body. "Are you going to say this wasn't consensual tomorrow?" she asked. Her fingers squeezed you even more.

"No," I said. There was nothing else to say, even though all of us knew it wasn't true.

The next day she tried to kiss me again and I dodged her. She punched the wall with her violinist's fist. The wall bowed and her knuckles bled and you ached in involuntary empathy. And I slept with her again, because I was so in awe of someone who could feel so strongly about me that she hurt herself. I kept sleeping with her. It was sick but it was only for a few weeks.

When I got home for the summer, I chewed and chewed those few weeks and decided that I had been sending her mixed messages. Maybe she was confused because of the breakup and the fact that we had kissed before. I deserved it for going up to her room in the first place. If I hadn't been so high, if I hadn't been dissociating, I could have wriggled out from underneath her. Even better, if I had just pulled you away from her that first time she grabbed you, everything would have been okay. One crisp snap of a movement and I could have never had to revisit the cracks mapped on her ceiling.

Oh how I blamed myself for hurting you (or vice versa).

But as often as I berated myself that summer for not actually walking out the door that night, I had the wonderful privilege of being physically removed from her. She could try to assert control over Skype and through letters, but she did not show up on my doorstep. Your bruises faded, your flesh swelled and shrank and swelled again. I was beginning to treat you better than she or I had been because I knew we were so lucky to be safe together. Occasionally I thought, haltingly, that we deserved someone who would not crush you to prove a point.

When I saw her months later, I would like to tell you that I stared through her, hard as an iced-tea spoon, and didn't speak. But I didn't. I tried to be friends with her, again, and in spite of your prickled-hair warnings. Sometimes we had fun with her, ghost-hunting in a group or making noodles in the dorm kitchen. But some nights she showed up to places where she knew I would be and sat glaring at me in the corner as I tried to pretend I wasn't scared. Other evenings I spent sitting stonefaced on the couch as she drunk-sobbed into my shoulder, telling me how badly I had treated her.

But you know that this happens, don't you? That the fact that everything is okay until it isn't makes it hard to leave? There are so many reasons why it is difficult to make a clean break, and I don't think I could have understood any of them without living through some of them.

I never told her I was cutting her off. I never spelled out to her how she had hurt me.

The closest thing that happened was this:

I went to a birthday party on a Tuesday night. Even though she wasn't invited, she showed up and found me and berated me for not telling her where I was going. When I told her that was none of her business, she grabbed you and my other arm and held you both against the wall. She was opening her mouth to yell again.

I thought of how the noise of a scream gives me more physical pain than the arm-hold she had me in. I thought of how I wished I could go back and yank you back from her that night months before. I thought of how I owed her nothing, not even my social calendar.

Or maybe I didn't think at all. Maybe it was an instinct that I'd been squashing that twisted you and my other arm out of her grip, fast as eels.

She stared at me.

I said: "You don't fucking touch me."

She hurt you for the last time that night, right forearm. I will defend you from anyone else who wants to hurt you and I will protect us from anyone else who tries to turn me against you. Though it took a while before I cut her out of my life entirely, I swear that she has not touched you or me again. She will never touch you again.
love,

To my representative, my ink:

You're an artificial product of the people who have touched my life. Everything that has ever happened to me and those I love is etched into my skin by you. Every life and body that has touched me is you and you are them. The first one of you that I got a few days after I graduated from high school represents the disappointment that I've been through. From past crushes and dead pets to people I thought I could rely on. You are a broken heart. You have represented all the upsets caused by people I had the audacity to think I could call "Dad" before I got you and after I got you. "Fool me once, shame on you. Fool me twice, shame on me." Never again, ink. We shan't be fooled again.

Thank you for representing me,

Letter to my heart

This has been a long time coming. I realized that you have had quite a difficult time dealing with all this stress. It's not that is didn't notice, It's that I failed to think about how important you are and how much I ignored you. You are part of me but you are still separate. I obviously never paid attention to you unless you were beating very quickly or were in distress. I noticed the physical pain associated with you. But that was just the physical aspect. So many years I spent time trying to make sure my story was true. I had to know that anything I told others was what I actually experienced. But what of you? I knew there was emotional pain too, but I choose to grant it value only in terms of what I experienced. I focused on the events. I am somehow engaging you now because I am crying. I don't even know how much of crying is autonomic and how much is emotional activation. I guess I have ignored you my whole life because that is what I learned I must do to survive. I had to keep a relationship with my parents and my emotions made them upset. I am not sure one could call it anger, but they made me feel there was something wrong with me if I could not just pick up and move on with out any affect. I wonder if I betrayed you as much as I felt betrayed by my parents? I can use the word feel or rather felt easily in my wording or expression but is it just a filler word or a figure of speech. Do I really feel that loss at all? Do I even know how? It seems like everything I am saying is so hollow. If my own heart does not merit my attention then what else am I missing? What else am I ignoring? Do I pay attention to the other messages my other body parts send to me. Is it like the post office who loses a letter for twenty years and then all of a sudden you have it delivered. I don't mean you as in the actual heart making sure I get the message twenty years later but then again as I am twice that age then maybe I was more correct than I had thought. How long have you been trying to get me to pay attention? Have I gone through times when I was more adept or aware than I am now, or I mean recently? Now that I am asking the questions are you going to hold back or are you so pleased that I am asking that you overflow with all this data that you have had to shove back on that shelf to protect me from myself? Now that I am here I am so confused. I don't even know where to go with this. I feel like I need a break. I feel so overwhelmed with the possibilities. I will seek to stay open to all that you can share but I ask you to let it go at a pace I can attenuate. All this information is gushing and part of me is still holding back. I am sensing a growing pain in my head as the largeness of this task is taking hold. I wonder if this is something that I can deal with as I have had so much stuff as data or information to make sense of or if this is a latent adaptation that I must be able to bring other areas of my body together with some sort of order or compatibility. I feel I need to say I am sorry, but is that sorry cognitive or is a real feeling? I can't say as I know. This is hard. I don't know that I was ready to open this door. I know I have opened pandora's box and I have no excuse for not seeing this through. I wish I had a teacher or guide to know what I am to do with all of this. I don't I have only to pause and ask GOD for some sort of order or direction, peace. There are so many other descriptors that I cannot cognitively get a grip in them. I hope I don't need to know all those other words or terms or whatever to make peace with my heart, with you. For someone who made a cognitive choice to feel my feelings when my grandfather died, or rather after, I don't know that I gave full attention to anything that felt like a feeling. I wish there was some other word to use other than felt. It does not convey the essence of what is traveling through my mind. The English language seems to fall so very short of describing what feelings are actually being animated. I am going to have to draw this letter to a close so that I have time to process. Please excuse me until I can put things together and understand this in a holistic way. Maybe it will be a fuller scope or sphere with some time. Time? More time. I don't like having to give this more time. I would like to clear it all up right now. There is a definite struggle between the cognition of what this "looks" like and the other aspects that have to do with feelings. Please find a center where the conflict can end. Would love to be able to say I love you but I can't. I want to know what love is, I hope you can show me. I hope I can "listen". I doubt very much that you have not offered me answers or suggestions. I have never been one to listen to you. I believed you needed to listen to me. I was in charge. Maybe I still am. I don't feel in control. I feel very much out of control. Can we call a truce. I will give you room to express but you need to give me room to acquaint myself with these new ideas/problems. Did you say promises? What do I need to know about promises? . . . I need to explore promises. I don't need to make promises, because I don't believe in them.? It seems you know me better as a cognitive being than I know how you function to make me a feeling being. As long as I seek to be a being, I am OK? I needed to know that. I choose to feel more and provide you with an outlet to release all that you have been holding. So for now we are good? I give you permission to send me messages if I fail to pay attention. Please not too painful.

Dear body, once a long time ago, you were paired with another, in a heavenly grace – a sum much greater than all of our parts together. So I will tell you a story about that time. It all began with our right-hand ... well, I should say 'my' right-hand and Sam's left-paw. His body and ours were in their usual position, snuggled as close as we could get to one another. No air or light could pass between us and our bodies so close – only true love.

Sitting gently on top of my small right-hand was his furry left-paw. My kitten's own left-hand. Smaller than mine, soft, and much more beautiful. Sam was his name. But there was so much more to how our bodies knew one another. In the deep green of Sam's eyes was a thin band of gold circling both of them. Just like my eyes. Except, Sam's eyes were happier. He had a slight mewing to his purr that sounded just like the song my lungs sang when I lay next to him. My heart beat too fast – that was different than Sam's, whose heart beat slow and content, full with promise. We both had fingers and toenails – Sam's were sharp and pointy at the tips, but he never scratched me. Mine were jagged and chewed down. Sam's downy coat was natural and always smelled clean. My hair was greasy and did not smell very good at all. The children at school even told me so when they laughed and held their noses as I hurried past them in the hallways and on the school playground.

Sam's movements and his legs – all four, were quick and confident – not hasty and unsure like my arms and legs. His did not quiver or shake like mine ... not until he became very ill. This was when our bodies became far too much alike but not in the sweet sensual way they used to be. Instead, our bodies; all the way past the skin and fur and down to the bone – became one body. One with an ugly sinister illness that would rack our frail bodies and make them seem singular. Like Siamese kittens attached and sharing one of every organ. The only difference was the he was a little kitten and I was a little boy.

His illness had come on suddenly, and it was his illness that showed us both how our bodies knew one another very well. Like they had met before, they would grow together and die together. But I did not know then, that one of us would win this terrible race. No victory medal to the winner. Only loneliness to the one left behind. And to the one left, his [my] body would remain ill. I would wish that in all the races I had lost until Sam, this would be the last that my body would lose – and fall, never to get up again – so that I was not only like my only friend in body, but with him forever in all ways.

It was Sam's once downy fur, now soaking wet all of the time that told my heart he was sick. I mean really sick. His slender body grew thin as the days passed when the mysterious illness appeared. At first, his eyes, a quiet green and gold, began to look sleepy. His small head drooped more often when he stood and he now seemed to always labor to stand these days. Sam's pretty coat used to be warm to the touch of my hands, but now it was cold and damp. There was now much more distance than there ever was between the floor and his light gray dark-spotted belly. But the worst of it was when his whole body shook and convulsed until Sam staggered, fell to the dirty carpet or linoleum, and the mewing turned to weak whimpers. A sound that was like feeble begging escaped his tiny throat and mouth. A mouth that once wore a perpetual smile now frowned and forced itself open for the smallest bites of what food I could find and share with him.

When Sam's body went into its spasms, so did mine and we fell to the floor together. My eyes wept, my own mouth quivered, my body ached with fear, and I begged and begged for someone – anyone to save him. Curling up next to Sam at night, our bodies sweat together, stunk of death, and loneliness. A piece of still life was all my mind and heart hung on to and soon I was feeding him with the same eye-dropper I used when he was a newborn. That which once gave him life now was used to try and save it.

Oh, my dear sweet friend. Our minds, hearts, and bodies are linked in life and death. *'You die … I die,'* I thought, every time I cried while watching Sam's tiny ribcage move far too slowly up and down while he lay on one side. His small face staring into mine – so close I could smell through my nose the little remaining sweet-scented breath. A breath like honey that always put me to sleep. When Sam was facing me, he was like a mirror of what my mind told me I had become. How I must have appeared to others: a cold resolve giving off the odorous wafts of weakness and fear.

I disciplined my body to take Mother's abuse. All of its ugly kinds; especially, the sex stuff. I could train my body to respond to Mother in order to avoid a beating that would come if I did not make her orgasm – and I trained my body not to respond to the strangers, making them bored, frustrated, and then finally, give up and blissfully leaving me alone. But I could not train my body, mind, and heart to react any other way to Sam dying except dying myself. When his body became unable to lift itself –mine too became paralyzed from the waist down. Pug, my little sister by two years, used all the strength in her even smaller body than mine, to work together with me just to get me to the toilet. Pug pulled, I dragged, and we both panted hot air from undersized and overworked lungs that lived inside of two malnourished children. I often wondered how Pug being so small, her body so ill, her heart so big … could pull me along the floor no matter how light I had become. Sam was easy to carry, even for me. But Pug's body harnessed the strength of Superman. The same strength used when my sickly weak body pulled Mother from drowning in a tub while she was naked, passed out, and heavy as an anchor. Sometimes, I asked my body where it got this strength to do such things, but it only kept quiet. As quiet as Sam as he laid sweating, dying, and trying to look like he was still smiling despite everything. Our wet eyes met.

In vain I suffered to save Sam. *"There's got to be a little life left in him,"* I prayed with every inch of me. "Just a little." But there was none and the time grew near. Generating a force of love behind every effort destined to be the one which saved Sam, my body – most particularly, my brain and heart, found nothing but failure. Mother and Father told me we did not have the money to save him, but they always had the money for cigarettes and alcohol.

My body's relationship with Sam could be seen in my eyes, hands, and mouth most often when I stared at him for hours, weeping and praying, touching his frail body as gently as I could, and singing the old tunes I once sang for him under the apple tree that stood in our yard.

The world we knew was slipping away, and now only our hearts fought together when our bodies and minds gave up long ago. As I lay another night with Sam's bony spine against my sunken tummy, a distant outline raised itself in my heart: Every stroke of my hand down his skeletal body would be the last. With great effort, Sam would raise his head to look back at me as we lay down and my ears cried when they heard his slight neck creak and crack. This was the effect our hearts had in comparison to one another. That and a prayer – for a God still sleeping to please let me follow Sam to the place he was soon to go.

I would return home one day from school. It was the last day of school before summer, and my lungs burned from running the whole way. This would be the first day in a succession of many, my mind said, where we would nurse Sam back to health, or at the very least, be there with him when he left … and if God was awake – I would go too. But when I walked into the only home I had ever known – Sam was gone. His whole body was nowhere to be found. Mother would not tell me where. My mind screamed, *"Now! Would be a good time to kill her. Now! Would be a good time to finally make all the wrongs – right again."* But my mind, like my body, was weak, and it shut its mouth and gave over to my heart which only wept in silence. My heart would not even tell my eyes, so that they would not show Mother was it was thinking. This would have only brought on a beating my body was too exhausted to withstand. *"It would come soon enough,"* my mind said.

Then it hit me like falling into stone that I would no longer hold him in my puny boy's arms. My mind and heart not even knowing what came of him in an already fragile world. I remember walking from Mother and seeing her bitter face stare only at the dirty blood and alcohol stained living room carpet. I walked into my bedroom on legs which had regained feeling from their temporary paralysis only a couple months ago. That feeling was somehow gone again, even though I was now able to walk. I fell on my pee-stained bed – the same one where bad things happened and were done to me, while always hoping Sam would not walk in and see.

There would be tears from eyes too tired to cry any longer. And from a hollow heart, presenting a picture of days with the only friend I ever had, were the distinctly marked memories of a rundown and broken dream living inside a brain that did not know what to do next. And a heart which now returned to the consciousness of knowing only abuse without reprieve.

"Oh aching heart, in the quiet looming of my mind, I was no more than a servant and would no longer hear the motor of the kitten I had once had, to give me peace."

Knowing God would not answer the prayer, every part of me still prayed for many nights afterwards that Sam would come back and take me with him. To that better place. That place where my heart was already waiting for my broken mind and body to finally catch up.

Instead, my body did as it always ... it lay on my bed and cried, desperately wishing Mother was just playing a cruel joke and Sam was hidden somewhere in the house. He was not. Not knowing how he died made it worse. It was important to me that he did not suffer in the end. It became difficult to keep Sam within my thoughts – within a mind relentless in its pursuit of insanity – without the anger interfering and pushing away the images of his playful character.

Several nights were spent lying awake and trying to remember him. My brain struggled for the perfect picture. Daydreaming about what he once was by closing my eyes and concentrating. Squeezing my eyes shut while doing so until they hurt and I saw the white dots floating in the pool of black.

My mind would hold the image of him for a few seconds, and then it would disappear, but not before I glimpsed his small face slipping slowly away in front of my solitary deserted and desolate eyes.

Sam's body was gone. Mine was wasted and still here. My heart, mind and soul told me over and over that Sam was the lucky one. This gave all of our parts great comfort. So, while my tender skin pricked and still burned where Mother threw the lit matches that stuck sometimes in order for me to stop crying over Sam – I hated my body. I hated it so much I wish I could give it all back to wherever it came.

Dear brain,

I dont use this word lightly but...I HATE you. For a long time I thought I hated my body, perhaps it was my fat, my imperfect skin, perhaps it was even the fact that my boobs couldnt even be perfect (with one almost a two size difference and floppy and the other well...just kind of there with no 'sex appeal')

None of that matters now though. Because now as I stare into this mirror and look into my eyes, eye's that I had also blamed for betraying me. I realize that no...it was never the fat or my eyes or anything other then you brain. You take residence in my body, in our only one true home and you betray me by filling my head and heart with words of self hate and disgust...silent torture.

Why?

Were you always this way? I can't recall a time were I felt beautiful...good. Maybe you started as a whisper when we were young, when the bodies of the woman we idolized both on the tv and in real life became thinner and thinner and eventually completely unattainable. Perhaps the whispers began to grow louder when Mom a wonder woman in our eyes brgan to morf into a hidious person because thats all she would say she was...and how could we not think of ourselves in the same way when we are one in the same as her.

I hate you. Im in so much pain brain. You whispers have grown to ear ringing screams to the point where I dont want to be here some days...your killing us, mentally and psyically. There are days wheb you've had me convinced that if I cut myself fat would pour oout i.stead of blood...but you're wrong brain...its always blood.

When does the madness end? When will you be satisfide? Are you in pain too brain? Are you just as tired as I am? I hope so, because I've fou.d someone who loves me for me, she thinks Im beautiful....crazy huh?

She's slowly starting to take away our fun house mirrors, and replacing them with ones that are real. Have you quieted down recently? Maybe Im just getting used to your crys.

I've written you this letter for a reason brain. Someday I will have a child, and when that day comes I refuse to have them feel anything you've made me feel. We have alot of work to do you and I. Alot of changing to do.

So let me start.

I love you brain.

To my Heart,

You are a Survivor!! Strong and Pumping Blood through my Body. When Mommy died, I was so sad, we hurt but you kept beating. When Daddy kicked me out of the house at 15, I was so afraid and scared you beat faster and you pumped stronger and we became stronger and stronger. We learned to Survive. I was so young and had a baby, just a teenager, a baby myself, but you kept beating, stronger, each beat, stronger, Survivors, you and me together.

The years of aging, years of pain, years of fear, years of sadness, hurt, years of disappointments. They were so long and so agonizing. But we grew stronger and stronger. We Survived. You pumped faster and stronger, and we learned to Survive through whatever life threw in our Face.
Then One day Happiness Finally Came!!! I finally found Happiness. You could finally be happy Heart. You were swept away, no more fear, no more sadness, no more pain, just Love and Happiness. Love after so many years of Pain. But it came at price. He rode in Like a Prince on a White Horse and swept me up into his arms of safety and Love. Like a Story Book, but with my Prince on his Horse, came a rider behind him, a tormenter. But we are Survivors, and Stand Firm we did. Our Love for Him is so strong, you have to start to beat hard again, you must pump strong again, Survive Damn it! Damn It! SURVIVE!!

He is ripped away from me with sickness. I watched him struggle with each and every breath. I hurt , I hurt, SURVIVE!! SURVIVE!!! Pain, Hurt!!! Damn it, Heart now you ache, you can't pump. You can't be strong anymore. You are finally broken and shattered into a million pieces. You are shredded like a knife has slashed you. Every beat hurts. He fights so hard, his Death bed wish " You are Survivor, Promise me you will live".

So once again Heart, we must beat and pump and Survive. I must take you on another journey. This one more painful than any before. The pain is not over, the Rider behind still torments, but he will not be allowed to cause us anymore pain. Because we are SURVIVORS.

TO MY HEART

I was dumb
Mistakes were made
But I will never
Let myself fade

I guess that
We were both wrong
For as it happened
You did sing that song

I wanted the happiness
I didn't want the pain
But I guess for a rainbow
There's has to be rain

I'm sorry for the aches
I'm sorry for the pain
I'm sorry for the sorrow
It won't happen again

Heart to Brain to Heart

"Hey! I said . . . Hey"!" My mouth spoke to my brain in no more than a raspy whisper. "You are giving away too many secrets."

But it was too late, my ears heard the words loud and clear, and that meant the strange man did too. In the night, with the slice of silver light coming through the dirty living room window, his cold and wet mouth wrapped itself around my privates just before he promised it wouldn't hurt. But his mouth lied and so did his floating glazed-over eyes. And when his throat started to gurgle and make that sucking sound, my stomach lurched, rolled, and then my own throat opened up and what little food was in my stomach from the past two-days came up and splashed all over his screaming red and bald head.

"Is this dirty?" my dry mouth whispered because there was no more air left in my lungs.

The man did not answer. His dry sandpaper lips and cold spit-filled mouth just kept sucking. Not only were his lips prickly, but they were big as if swollen, stiff like the lump in his pants that his right-hand rubbed sometimes, and quick. Too quick. His whole head moved back and forth in these jerking motions, and every time the man snapped his head forward, his bristly hairy chin punched my small and undersized testicles. My brain was trying to figure out what was worse – the bad things the man was doing to my private parts or the pain. I think my brain finally gave up and said to me that both were the same. A "tie" we called it when we raced in the schoolyard. My legs never knew what a "tie" felt like because I was too small, hungry, and slow.

My heart told me what the man was doing is dirty and told my brain not to tell anyone. Not the man for sure, but not anyone – ever. My heart wanted to make sure, so it said to my brain, *"You promise?"*

And my brain answered the same it always did in that tired, 'I give up, you win,' kind of way.

"I promise."
Then my brain told every other part of me – head to toe, it was dirty, and to keep it to myself. My heart jumped in like it always did and said to the brain, *"Hey, you are tricking us!"*

But the brain said that some of the money Mother got would be for food and suddenly had my tummy on its side. Still, my mouth 'sometimes' never listened to my brain. Mother said that all that time. So, my mouth asked the man again … *"Is this dirty?"*

Too bad for me that both his ears did not work, because he did not seem to hear me. My small and ten-year-old penis hated this feeling and told the man's mouth by staying asleep. Even if my brain and heart did not agree with one another, my penis did not care. It knew that when every now and then it would get a little bigger, the stranger's lungs would fill with air and it was always hot against my belly. The strangers would try harder and stay longer. So, my penis stayed asleep but this was not difficult. My brain, heart, and penis liked working together when it came to the strangers.

The man was pushing his puffy face against my tummy and then his whole mouth opened up really wide and he swallowed all of my privates. Faster and faster his head rocked back and forth.

My brain said, *"He is not slow and careful like the older neighbor girl who sometimes babysat us."* But my heart didn't care because that too felt just as dirty and one time my eyes closed really tight but the tears squeezed through anyway. The older neighbor girl did not even look up to see, but the tears fell on her open breasts that embarrassed me to look at. My eyes opened long enough to see her hand pressing one of her bare 'titties' as my brother called them, and her other hand was down her panties in the front. My brain and eyes knew what was down there. It was her privates and her hand did not seem to care if it was pressing too hard and maybe hurting her. I did not care either because she did not care about the tears my eyes sent her, with a secret message from my brain and heart that she should stop and go home.
The man's throat made a grunting noise like a pig. Like a pig that was mad at the other pigs.

My little arms were so heavy all of a sudden, and I had to tell my brain to tell my arms to lift up and at the same time 'cause I needed both of them to do what seemed to my brain like a good idea – tell my hands, now really numb, to push the man's forehead backward. But his forehead was slippery and sweating even though it was winter and the electricity was shut off in the house, making it cold all the time.

The man's breath was panting like a thirsty dog and my ears warned my brain you better tell our hands to hurry because the man was trying to hurry too. My penis tried to stay asleep, but sometimes it would wake up but my brain told it to go back to sleep again. My back hurt because it was stiff and ached from standing too long and trying not to fall down. My brain warned me many times that I did not want to lay down. That would be dangerous. More dangerous.

The bad feeling in my heart helped my penis stay sleepy. The man's eyes went from looking happy to angry. Again, my brain told my heavy arms to tell my hands to push a heap harder against the man's sweaty forehead. But his own brain, body, arms, and hands must have been telling him to try harder and to hurry. Because that is what he did.
Suddenly, my throat got really small and I was choking. My eyes watched what little vomit was on the top of the man's head and the floor, but the man did not care. He did not even get sick like my brother did when I puked in front of him. When I did that, my brother's stomach gave up what little food it had inside it too.

My eyes could not find anything to stare at in the room, and so they started to close while my head seemed to grow really big and too heavy for my thin neck to hold up. And, the fading light got darker all around me.

My mouth said, "I want to go to bed," to the man, but his ears were still not working. His hands worked pretty good because his left-hand grabbed my naked bum and was as big as one of my cheeks. The man's other hand told his thumb and his 'pointy finger' to hold my penis and squeeze it. His hand also told those two fingers to pull and then push really hard past the man's ugly teeth that were yellow from smoking like Mother's. But her teeth were not real.

My brain, my body, my penis, everything – hurt really bad. Not the kind of hurt my heart felt, but that kind of hurt was there too. Mostly, it was like when my legs ran until they could not run anymore but had to keep running so they were shaky.
It was when my brain remembered my heart again that I started to pray. I did not use my mouth, but the one I kept on the inside that lived in my head and first prayed to the moon. While the man's stubbly face decided it was time to scratch my belly and inside of my legs. My brain said the man's face was doing this the whole time but forgot to tell me.

I prayed to the birds I could barely hear outside because it was nighttime and they were going to sleep. Not sleepy like my penis to be safe – but in the good way. Because their bellies told their mouths that told their beaks that told their throats to eat the bugs and worms that filled their bellies, and now the bird's bellies told their brains it was time to sleep. My brain and heart both agreed that it was good to be a bird. Especially now. Any kind of bird – a crow, goose, an eagle to carry me away or an owl to sing me a lullaby.

The man's hands, fingers, arms, and body finally gave out. Even his knees which cracked, with a popping noise that came from one of them as he shifted his weight and struggled to stand. His eyes squished shut when one of his knees cracked and he bent over again very fast. He then stood up straight. My own eyes stared at the floor. My brain was too afraid to tell my arms to tell my hands that they should pull up my large hand-me-down dirty underwear. The man's throat grunted again and he wobbled on short and fat legs that carried him out the battered front door.

It wasn't until the door shut behind him that my neck turned and forced my eyes to look into the cracked mirror over a cardboard bookshelf. The mirror played a trick on my eyes because it was broken, and my brain saw two faces. Both faces were reflected in the mirror – only one was good enough to see, and only if I closed my right or left eye. My brain could not remember which eye I needed to close for a better look at the mirror. But then for some reason my brain told the eye that could not see as well to close and I saw my face. It was white like a ghost and puffy from crying. The one eye staring back at me was round like a Frisbee and red. My penis ached and it felt like there was wet poison all over it eating through the skin.

The man's work was done but he would be back tomorrow and my brain and heart told me this. But they did not need to – because I could see Mother's crooked mouth in my mind making sure I remembered the man would be back. Just then, Mother yelled from her bedroom for me to get in bed.

My body would not listen, and it took Mother's angry crooked mouth a second time to make my body move. It did slowly and I crept past the opening of Mother's door as quietly as I could even though my brain knew she was awake. My eyes and ears did too.

It was dark but my eyes said they could find my doorway, so they told my hands to reach for the old molding to the bedroom I shared with my brother. Once they found it, I stumbled to the bed on my feeble legs and lay next to my brother's warm body. My ears listened to him breathe and this made my body very tired, my head heavy, and my heart lonely.

Before falling asleep, my brain told me to shut my eyes. But my heart told me it wanted to be a bird before I woke up the next day.

Dear Heart,

I know you're hurting, I can feel the pain. Right now you feel like a piece of paper that got crumpled up and thrown aside. Over time, I've been straightening that paper out. It may have some rips, and some creases can't be completely straightened out, but you're healing. It may not be tomorrow, it may not be next month, but you are growing stronger and stronger every day. You've already gotten through the hardest part and that is recognizing the strength you have as a person, and knowing you deserve nothing but the best.

You're doing a great job.

Love,

Your inner strength.

Dearest smile,

I miss you. It has been one year, eleven months, and ten days since the last time I saw you. Now, when I look in the mirror, I see a reflection I don't know; a product of circumstance. I know exactly where I left you. I know exactly when I left you.

I'm sorry I fell asleep in his bed. I'm sorry I stopped eating. I'm sorry for covering my body in scars. I'm so sorry I left you in that dark apartment at 3:48 in the morning.

I realize that I will never get my virginity or innocence back. I know the friends I've lost will not come knocking at my door. And I know that he will never fully understand what he did. But if I could have any of it I would just want you to appear across my face once again. I want something back.

Please come back to me.
I miss you.

Affectionately yours,

Dear ~~lips~~,

Dear lips,

    For years I refused to let you smile. You
~~&~~ were only allowed to frown or be expressionless.
You are beautiful, full, and pink. From this
point on I am giving you freedom to show
off that smile. I will paint you in any
shade you desire. Protect you from the
sun and keep you from harm. I will
wake up every morning and look at you
in the mirror until you decide which
angle you will choose to go. Whether
it ~~&~~ be a frown or a big kool aid
smile. I am never going to let someone
else decide for you again. I love you.

When I Say Cunt, You Tell Me I'm Crass

Women used to go to parties. They would hold mirrors up to you, investigating your folds, trying to understand you.
But looking is not enough. A mirror will never tell you the truth.

This is mine. You are mine.
I thought for longer than I care to admit that you were his.
He asked me to open up for him, and I did.
He told me you belonged to him.
He said he created us for this purpose, and I believed him.

I am done apologizing.
I do not hold the blame for this, for the things he put inside you.
This is not our fault. I am done pretending. I am done with silence.

There are names for you that I love.
Cunt.
Axe wound.
Taco.
Vag.
Slit.

None of these words are quiet.
None of them sound gentle and feminine.
I don't believe in gentility.
I do not believe in femininity.

These words are difficult to hear.
They are violent and carry with them the blood of my lifetime.
I call you cunt. I call me cunt. And this is a moment of truth.

Dear Heart:

When I was little, I used to have this thing with paper napkins. If there was one in front of me, it couldn't be allowed to just lie there. Instead, I was strongly compelled to lay it out flat and then run my palm over it, again and again, until it was totally smooth. No ripples at all. I did the same thing with bed sheets. Every night before I climbed between the sheets, I had to take my hand and smooth it out. There couldn't be a wrinkle at all. Not in the paper napkins and not in the bedsheets. They had to be smooth, clean. I was usually too uptight at bedtime to really think about the reasons but, during the day, I pretended the napkins were hurt and I was erasing the pain by smoothing the wrinkles out. I've never really stopped, actually. Even today, when someone gives me a napkin, my first impulse is to smooth it out. Every night, before I slide between the cool sheets of the bed, I run my hand over them, careful not to lay on any wrinkles.

I have a character in my head. She's young with an Indian-like complexion. Her nearly black hair slides over her cheek and she keeps her head down. When she raises her eyes to look at me, they are beautiful---but dark and shuttered. She is wearing a simple, dirty, white, cotton dress. I don't know why yet but I know she is traumatized. Traumatized to the point of silence. She doesn't speak, I have no idea what her name is. I don't know her story, either, although I have a dismal inkling. What I do know is that she makes me very, very sad. Usually, the presence of a new character excites me and fills my every core with anticipation. I am excited to see this new girl---but she makes you hurt.

You've known the breathless agony of gut-wrenching pain for nigh on twenty-seven years. The start of the school year is a "trigger" for us, if ever there was one. Children starting school, bright faces showcasing eager minds. New backpacks, pencils, paper, colorful crayons and markers, folders with cute pictures. *Hope*. Hope for the future so clearly defined in the shining eyes of youth. I remember being excited about going "back to school" shopping. But the first day of school inevitably terrified me. Instead of rejoicing in hope for new friends and bright beginnings, it was a time when you squeezed painfully inside my chest. While others were learning to share secrets with their peers, I was learning to build walls around you because I knew time was limited. I

67

couldn't afford to let you get close to friends we were going to leave in a few months' time because another loss would have broke you again.

I remember that first terrible, terrible night. It's ironic that I can write about it in fiction so eloquently and yet, here, in this personal space of a journal, I hesitate. Sometimes.... sometimes, I would lie there and pretend it wasn't me at all, I was just watching the life of the current character unfold. Your beating would become labored because I wouldn't breathe right; *breathe in and hold it.... hold it... hold it..... exhale slowly... repeat.* Controlling my breathing forced me to focus on you. I could feel you beat....*thump....thump...thump.* That first terror-provoking night, what I remember the most is a series of violent actions which is funny, because he wasn't violent that first night. He was calm and quiet; soothing even, almost, in a demented sort of way. His hands bothered you the most.

Hands are supposed to be gentle. Hands are supposed to soothe. But they didn't. And then, by the time it was over, pain racked my body. I was crying of course. I cried at the drop of a hat those days. But you... you were beating so fast, almost as thought you were trying to catch up with the thoughts in my head. The tears were making me hiccup and choke. I think it was the fights I'd heard before, I'm not sure, but somehow I knew to focus on my breathing. I did that and you slowed down. I don't remember what I did the rest of that night, frankly. I don't remember if I prayed, if I went to the bathroom or if I just cried myself to sleep. After the sheets were gone, everything is a hazy, uncertain fog.

But you were never the same.

It's been twenty-seven years since you've taken a rest. It's been twenty-seven years since you've beat normally. Doctors say your erratic; they diagnose me with tachycardia. Then they found a hole in you; a hole that caused two TIAs---mini strokes. A hole that was quite literally endangering my very life. They wanted to bandage it---in essence, they put a band-aid on you. For weeks after that surgery, I sobbed. You had been through so much and I had spent so long trying to keep you safe. But, somehow, a hole, a literal one, punctured our walls. I remember laughing with the pre-op nurses as I took the pre-surgery tests. But then, as I was rolled into the operating room, I got nervous. They injected some "sleep medicine" into my hand and I went to sleep.

But I awoke a few minutes later, when they had such trouble finding a vein they were seeking one in my neck. I was crying, but I didn't know why, and a nurse patted my hand, said, "It's okay" and the next thing I knew, I was out again. When I awoke, I had twelve holes in my neck and a band-aid on you.

I was "healed."

And even though that wasn't really true, I tried so hard to make it so. I jumped headfirst into the daytime and, at night, I left a bathroom light on and counting my breaths until I went to sleep. I've tried to shield you with walls. I'm pretty good at blocking emotion from truly hitting you. I cry more because I'm exhausted than because of emotional pain these days. But sometimes I find a crack in the wall. Like when school starts and I remember that, once upon a time, there was a five-year-old starting Kindergarten whose name was Tiffini. Sometimes I think of when our lives were in danger and only the grace of God got us all out. Sometimes a character comes along, like Anna or Taya or this new, as-of-yet-unnamed girl, that strikes right where the crack in our defense is. This woman I talked to at a signing recently said to me with tears in her eyes, "I feel like I know you." And my face flushed; I stammered the point where she tried to apologize. But I shook my head and admitted, "You do know me. And I am so sorry." This perfect stranger and I hugged and, for just a second, I wasn't the Advocate and Author; I was the little girl again.

Sometimes, dear Heart, what I wish is that I could take you and hold you in my hands and really, really look at you in a way that very precious few people have ever done. When I did, I'd see the wrinkle caused by the hurt that came every time he gave me a gift. When I did, I'd see the wrinkle caused by the hurt that came every time he kissed me. When I did, I'd see the wrinkle caused by the hurt that came every time I left potential friends. When I did, I'd see the wrinkle caused by the loss of fire. When I did, I'd see the wrinkle the loss of family caused. When I did, I'd see the wrinkle caused by every terrifying reason I can't sleep. When I did, I'd see the wrinkle of torment caused by learning he told other inmates his daughter was his girlfriend. When I did, I'd see the wrinkle caused by the word cancer after finally reclaiming a little joy.

And, ever so gently, I'd use my fingers to smooth each wrinkle. I'd use the memory of the birth of each of my daughters to smooth out two lines of hurt. I'd use the softness of a rose petal to smooth the wrinkle created by a rough hand and body. I'd use the snapshots of beauty taken at Cade's Cove and Georgia to smooth the hurt of the interstate. I'd use the warm conversations with genuine friends to smooth the hurt caused by neglect. I'd use the verses of Scripture that lulled me to sleep as a child to smooth the hurt caused by words. One by one, I'd ever so gently smooth your wrinkles just like I did on the napkins and the bedsheets. I'd finally see all the places you've been crumpled and torn and would smooth the hurt with a gentle touch. No, I couldn't erase it. The wrinkles don't really disappear, they just move. I know. But I'd wager a hefty sum that a genuine touch of love, one free from obligation and expectation, would go a long way to making you feel whole again. You've been in a state of breathless agony for a long time. At first, you were waiting on a knight in shining armor. Then you were waiting on an instantaneous miracle from God (which might still happen, by the way). Then you stopped waiting on others and started waiting on me.

I know you are.

I'm not so far disconnected that I don't understand that that's what this nameless character, and all the others like Anna and Taya and Abrielle, have been about. I know that's what the dreams are about; your way of trying to push me into action. I just don't know what action that is, as of yet. To tear down the walls. The thought paralyzes me; after so long spent guarding you, what would I do if some idiot ripped you apart? Still, I know you're waiting.

And I guess I'm writing because I wanted you to know I'm trying.

Frankly, the thought of writing whatever story this new character wants me to write is mind-numbing in its terror. I have an inkling of what it is. I've been goaded into enough research that I'm pretty sure I know the general direction she's going to take. And I don't want to write it, for whatever its worth. But I will. Because, once upon a time, I made you a promise. A promise to protect you from here on out. A promise to never let anything hurt you like that again.... not even memory.

God's not done with me--or you, dear Heart--yet. And sometimes the journey to "heart-happiness" is filled with bumpy dirt roads and mountains of dangerous terrain. Sometimes it's filled with dead-ends too. But, truly, once and for all, know that you can rest assured. You can trust; that's not been stolen. You can love; nothing proves that as beautifully as what you feel when you look at Breathe and Alight. You are not *broken*; you prove that every time you get excited about something that's yet to happen, like last night when you bought the first two Christmas presents in August. And you can heal; you do every time you speak to other survivors, every time you pray, every time you play with the girls and every time you write.

Love,
Me

Dear Eyes,

You've seen him, better than any other part of me, be so kind and so gentle and so loving. You've looked into his eyes and seen so much love for me.

You've seen him. You know he's not as strong as I am.

You also saw him hit me. You saw him laying in my bed and for a minute taking out his frustrations on me. You saw him continue to lay there, no obvious regard for the pain he had just inflicted on someone he claimed to love.

I know you hate to cry, that you don't like to feel unmanly. But I understand why you needed to cry so hard that night. And I want you to know it doesn't make you unmanly. You had had so many conversations with his eyes and you trusted him. Things had been hard between us, but I had trusted him too. I didn't expect to feel so hurt and betrayed and confused by him.

And the next day he wouldn't even look at you and you felt so guilty yet you felt manipulated too. You cried again and it all just felt bad, bad about him and bad about me. Later his eyes tried to tell you how sorry he was, but you didn't trust him because you had seen them so full of anger and aggression. And months later when I tried to bring it up once, his eyes flashed so full of anger at you and you had to see that directed at you again.

You've seen so much that hurt us, but I just didn't want to believe it all was real because I loved him so much. You were the eyewitness to all my worst moments after his betrayal too. I hadn't felt good about myself before the incident, but it just got worse. You were the only witness to my ensuing violence against my own body in my worst times of feeling lonely and worthless. It's not that I think that's his fault since it was my hand that held the razor blade, but also he made me feel just so worthless. The looks he gave you when I wouldn't cuddle or admitted I didn't feel like I could trust him were almost as painful as the day he hit me.

I know I should have saved you the tears by not going back to him the next week, even though I still loved him. I know I should have taken time away, so you didn't have to see him and see the replay of his aggression until you had at least stopped crying. And for that I am sorry.

Love always,
a kid who's just trying to move forward in his life

Dear Head,

Throughout your struggle as a victim, I want you to remember you are also a survivor. There is no reason you should feel the need to look down in embarrassment. There is no stamp or label on your forehead labeling you as a victim. You are not dirty, damaged, ugly, weak or stupid. Remind your brain you are not just another statistic. This is not, and never will be your fault. Stop looking down. You know where you are walking. You know where you are going in life, regardless of what he said, or someone else's opinion. They are not a survivor like you. It's time to hold your head high and with confidence. You are strong enough to move forward.

With love,

You.

A Letter to my Mouth:

You wait for and love the feel of the girls' kisses. Your tongue can make funky shapes. You absolutely love peaches. You don't say much, but you smile constantly. You love reading stories out loud. You are never adorned. You love the taste of chocolate on your lips and the act of singing. You're my mouth… but you're so much more too.

I've never really known how to handle you. I've never really known how to protect you. I've never really learned how to use you. I don't remember worrying about you when I was very, very young. Remember when we went with Papa and Grandmama to the Bahamas and you told them a funny story that Papa repeated for years and years? And, on that same trip, remember how, in the airplane, you asked Grandmama if our hands could open the window and grab a star to bring back to Mama? These are really the first memories I have of you. Probably because you were never used very much. Not nearly as much as you should have been. I don't know why, I think I was trying to keep all of us safe even before there was any real danger. And then It came. We were five years old and although I remember a lot of horrific things about that time, things that still make my insides swim and heart race, one of the most terrifying was what happened to you. Every part of you, from your lips to your tongue to your tastebuds, were affected. His mouth on you. It was wet and hard and scratchy. I jerked my head away, I remember that, but it didn't work. I remember using blankets to swipe over you so as to get the slobber off when I couldn't use my hands. Nobody ever thinks about the violence that happens to a mouth, do they? But when something is covering you, it affects the entire body's ability to breathe, and it can keep all of me still like nothing else can. You've always been a part of my body that I think of as…. special and…. fragile…. tender. You had to work so hard, for so long. I know it was hard on you, keeping still, not spewing out words that my self-control wouldn't let you say. I trained myself to breathe through you— small, short bursts of air that would keep the tears from falling. And you never said a word. I tried to protect you—I wouldn't even wear lip or chapstick because I knew you didn't want anything at all on you. People always talk about the affect abuse has on the rest of a body. I remember being utterly terrified all parts of my body were so damaged that I wouldn't be able to have children. All of those terrors and fears were real and valid. But even I overlooked and took for granted you. I thought, "It's just a mouth: it's there for eating." I never really imagined the kind of power you have. I never really gave you the credit you deserve.

Until one day....

One day, you were set free. Words I never thought you'd say spilled from you. You put truth into the air and changed my whole life dramatically. I was safe, finally, because of you. Because, when I thought I wouldn't have the words I needed, you said them anyway. When I thought I would stumble and trip and get choked up, you calmly acknowledged the past. I was afraid, and felt ashamed, but you spoke up. I used to look in mirrors while I sang. I was fascinated by how you form words. I wanted to see the shape of words. I wanted to know how you made sound. I thought of you as magical in a way——but I had never really believed you could help heal the heart. I expected a knight in shining armor to do that or maybe another pair of eyes that would see and race to save. Maybe, I thought, it would be a book that would somehow, someday, act as a saving grace. I thought I would just move out one day and everything would be forgotten. If I could just get us to adulthood, I thought, something supernatural and divine would then keep us safe. Funny, I never thought the power was on me the whole time. I never really believed anything you might say would stop it. But it did. You did. And not only did you tell it once, you've spoken in front of others too. Today, I think of how often you help me teach children at church and how often you say "I love you" to the girls. You're not just a part of my face; you've been an integral part of my life. Thank you for saying what needed to be said. Thank you for reassuring my girls of how much I love them, and am in awe of them.

I know you still aren't completely healed.

I still feel the need to tightly control what touches you, or what you're asked to hold or swallow. I still don't put make-up on you—no lipstick, no chapstick—because it makes you feel used and uncomfortable. That kiss, the one as a little girl, totally marked you and made you reluctant. Even today, a kiss is never simply a kiss. Fear starts knocking when anyone gets close enough to touch you. Maybe it always will. But....you have given me reason to hope, too, because of the time when a kiss didn't threaten my safety; when the touch of someone's mouth on you didn't make me jerk away or want nothing more than to wipe all evidence of touch off of you. Despite all the trauma you've ever endured, you can still feel warmth and sweetness and goodness. How strong are you.... you've known violence and shame, yet you've spoken out and retained the hope that whispers not all is lost. I used to fear I was broken. I used to fear you were broken. But if that was true, you'd never have been able to experience anything positive. The sweet taste of peach juice on the lip, the refreshing taste of water tickling your nerves, the healing balm of needed truth and the reassurance of a safe yet passionate, soft kiss.... all of these, you'd never have allowed yourself to feel if the pain still had you numbed. You've given me hope because you've shown me that you can be used as a tool for grace and compassion. You've reminded me that real beauty is natural. You've reminded me that words are all the more powerful when spoken instead of just being written. When you spoke up, I gained an entire support system I never would have known otherwise. My family and perfect strangers alike how used their mouths to tell their stories and you've been used to share mine. You've whispered prayers, you've laughed, you've shouted out "why?" and you've been still because you know there's a time for everything: a talk to time and a time to listen.

You hold a lot of memories. Good ones and terrifying ones alike. When I touch my fingers to you, the nerve endings jump because you are so rarely touched at all anymore. Maybe that's a good thing. Confidence, or the lack thereof, seeps into every pore of our skin. My hands are still cautious about touching anything. My muscles are still too fearful of danger to relax at night, even alone. And, sometimes, words still get stuck in the back of the throat, unable to find their way to the tongue and out of you.This is your time to how to speak whatever you want, without having to hold back. I've taken you for granted. I've thought of you as little more than a picture that's been pasted on with glue to make my face complete. In fact, I've sometimes tried to hide you by brushing my hair over the cheek until it almost covers you up. The smile you wear every day is also a form of cover-up. You know it because I can feel the muscles straining now when I couldn't before. You're tired. But know... This is your time to rest. This is your time to learn to trust touch again. This is your time to say what needs to be said, and the ears' turn to hear what needs to be said. I don't know what you'll saytomorrow or five years from now. I don't know what you'll have to feel, or what you may want to feel. But I do know that you are an essential part of my overrall healing and happiness. I know you are special. Did you know that the average kid laughs 400 times a day while the average adult only laughs about 15 times a day? But you... you have a special opportunity. When you were new, in my childhood, you laughed maybe fifteen times a day but today, as an adult, you are laughing much more—maybe as much as the average kid! Our days are full of so much adventure and I have learned so much about beauty and gratefulness and it all makes me want to smile and laugh more. That's a special thing; it means the danger is over. You can stop worrying about negative words and painful touch and instead start learning how to respond to positive words and positive touch. Your first instinct upon hearing praise of any kind is to dismiss it. How many times have you said, *"Oh, you'd be surprised"* with a self-deprecating laugh when someone complimented you? How many times have you muttered, *"Oh, I'm fine"* when I'm asked how I am? It's habit — I don't think about it anymore, it's just what comes out of you automatically. But the automatic words have an impact on my heart. Truth isn't only important about the big things—it's important about the little things too.

You've grown and matured so much these past 32 years. You're not nearly as frightened anymore—not of touch and not of truth. And I am proud of you.

A Letter to My Surgically Removed Breasts

How enticing you must have been for my ex-abuser to want to touch and molest...
How irresistible you were at age fifteen...
My abuser travelled across continents to gain access to them...
For 7 years, he did this...
Until I decided it was over...

20 years later, he stalked me because maybe he wanted to touch you again...
And I decided that it was still over...
And I was so afraid and confused about what had happened in the past...

Last year, you turned 45 and your biopsy showed LCIS...
A high risk condition...
High risk for turning into invasive lobular breast cancer...
And I decided that your power to entice was potentially cancerous...
And I cried because I had to let you go...
Because you could potentially kill me if I held onto you for too long...
Your power was silent and so overwhelming...
But I decided I wanted to continue to live, even though memories of the abusive past made me want to die somehow....

So I went to see the surgeon doctor with the nebbishy name...
And instead he turned out not to be nebbish-y at all...
In fact, he was a blond European prince with a shy look and long piano fingers....
He touched you, too,
Like he does everyday with dozens of other breasts...some more diseased than you...
And, stunned, I decided that he should remove you and replace you with silicone....
I signed the consent form...
I lay awake at night thinking if I would miss you...
And I thought I would miss watching my son grow up more....
So I steeled myself to go ahead with the surgery date...
And the handsome young blond doctor, who likes scuba diving,
Removed you, but kept your skin and your brown areolae...
And fit in silicone baggies in your place....

I woke up from surgery with a start...
And screwed my eyes to focus on the time on the clock on the wall...
Hours had passed...
And it felt like only fifteen minutes had gone by...
And you were gone...
Forever...
But I felt the swollen tender silicone mounds in your place...
And I pressed the PCA pump to get ahead of the upcoming pain...
And I just felt woozy...
And woozier...
And vomited over
And over....

I was up all night...
The TED stockings inflated every 15 minutes and kept me up....
The hospital PA system announced "Code Stroke" in some far away rooms on the other side of the hospital...
The fifth time it announced "Code Stroke" was in the room adjacent to mine...
I wanted to leave as soon as possible...

In the morning, at 6:40 AM, the blonde doctor knocked shyly on the door...
He came in dressed in green scrubs and a long charcoal wool coat...
He asked me how I was...
He said Naproxen was good for pain relief and swelling...
I showed him my wounds...
But I winced as I tried to snap up the shoulder of the hospital gown...
He gently and wordlessly snapped it together for me...
And I was grateful...
For that small act of kindness...

Other people have not always been so kind to you...
Or so respectful...
How strange such a small simple act
Could mean so much when I realized I lost you forever...
And, yet, I gained something else in return...
Sometimes when the blonde doctor looks at me...
I don't feel so bad about missing you so much anymore...
He looks at your silicone replacements...
And we both smile at each other...

And, suddenly, everything feels somehow okay again...
And sometimes I smile to myself even when blonde doctor is not around...
And I am okay.

Hello heart,

I knows it been awhile since I checked in. Its been 36 years since the first memory of abuse and we are still here. Its been a long a trying road...Even when we thought God didn't care He still had us...He had us when we tried to hide...He had us when we didn't give a FUCK anymore and He had us as we made our way back home. On this journey we have gone from disconnected to connected. We no longer have to live in crisis and try to save the world to be alive. We relearned what love and family means and who it is to be us. I know you have the little girl and teenager and they are healing. The bandages are removed. I can finally take care of them as the adult and they are protected. WE are finally one. They no longer have to take over to feel love from within. I am finally whole.

Family

What is it
It is hard to fit in
It is hard to blend
It is easier to remain unseen to go against my reasoning
But maybe...
If I try and show the real me
Maybe show what I could be
I will find the real meaning of family
I have finally found it. It is not those who say they love you and hurt you and make you believe you are worth nothing. It is those who will hold your hand and your heart and ask for nothing in return.

To my lips:

Zárva. Alva. Tudom, hogy jól.
We slept as innocently as our mother that left me home alone. She chose the man that liked my,

Puszi, pussy, my lips our lips, you carry stories that I carry no guilt in. The boy on Margit Híd stared and striped you down as you mouthed the words: My home hurt me and találtam egy újat. He could only see the blackness at the back of your throat. As someone that had never had his words bit back, he said your survival is wanting attention. He said that your survival doesn't, isn't, won't. Otthonom bántott és I found a new one.

I have no guilt in ezek az ajkak. They house my heavy and release my hurt. These are my stories, these are the words that I eat and bevesz. Nem bűnös. Nem bűnös, nem bűnös, just as the days you dreamed of sleeping innocently.

Puszi,

Dear 'Right Wrist,' I know you are only eight-years-old right now and you do not know how to read very well. But I have been meaning to tell you that I did not know a giant fat artery ran down the length of your soft belly. Nope, I did not know, but Mother did. Sometimes I wonder how she knew because she did not seem much smarter than me about things like that. When she drank and the bad things happened, she did not seem very smart or nice at all.

I remember how Mother made you show her your thin white belly and also the way she traced her fingers down the whole length of your upside-down arm. You were so scared but I remember you telling the brain that this sort of tickled and could be fun. That maybe, the brain said, it could be a new game. But then she showed you the knife. The one with the broken handle Mother always kept hidden under the cushion of the dirty couch. The knife was always dirty even though she never used it in the kitchen. Mother did not spend much time in the kitchen, but the brain said it was because there was no food. My stomach told me the same thing all the time.

We —all of us; the eyes, brain, heart, and 'you' right-wrist, realized that this was not a game. That Mother was in one of her moods and a really bad one, so you started to jump around and seemed to want to run away on your two weak, but friendly legs. Mother's own left-hand was awfully strong and her right-hand seemed to really like holding the knife and poking the tip into the pale skin where our wrist began just under the palm of our right-hand. Remember when the brain kept asking why was Mother staring a lot at the elbow?

Then the mouth screamed before the brain could answer. It was a familiar scream. The scream the mouth got really good at and even knew how to tell the lips when to pull back and tighten in a thin line. The teeth always helped by making this hissing noise.

The brain said, *No!* When all of a sudden the sad green and gold eyes both saw Mother smiling and showing us her own teeth which were fake. And the brain said, "*The teeth are not real and she is not real,*" but the pain was and the first stabbing motion pushed the dirty kitchen knife deep into your wrist; almost exactly in the middle, and then <other's stronger right-hand stopped.

Her left-hand then grabbed our elbow and held it very strongly. She now pulled the knife down your little belly, leaving a tiny trail of pink and red folds of skin. The path was very straight to begin with but I think Mother's brain lost concentration and the trail began to curve to the left, reaching half the distance between the beginning of your wrist and the end of that funny pocket in your arm where it can bend only one way. The brain then sent a message to the body that sometimes Mother made it bend the wrong way?

Oh poor wrist, now the under-side of your right-arm's belly is covered with a pretty red blood and my eyes can no longer see your skin because of its new liquid blanket.

That's when the whole body told the brain that it was not hot any more from the summer heat, but now getting both cold and sleepy. Mother let us lay down on the floor and then she stumbled away on her own not so strong legs. Not because they were a little boy's or weak from hunger, but because her mouth and stomach really liked the smelly alcohol.

Then Tina found us soon after because I remember her mouth talking to our ears and saying things that did not make sense to us, like; *"Tyler, don't die! Don't die!"* The brain thought Tina was silly to think that because we were not dying, we were just resting – all of us – every part of our body.

The towel Tina used to wrap around your small bicep, round and round, over the 'one-way bendy part' hurt every time she twisted it with something like a stick.

We, the body, did not mind any of this. Because Tina had carried us to the front porch and laid our thin body on the cool cement. Our eyes stared at the clear blue sky and the brain was too busy telling us that we were sleepy. While the heart told us that 'everything was going to be okay.' But our ears heard Tina crying and so my mouth told Tina what the heart was saying, but this only made her cry harder.

But it was okay. My body told me. It told me that we can rest for a while, and when we wake up, 'Everything is going to be okay.' The mouth said the words one more time, too quiet for the ears to hear, but the brain did.

And, finally while your soft belly pumped a pretty red color all over the towel and onto the now cold porch, with Tina rocking our head in her lap back and forth, the eyes closed and the mouth smiled before the most amazing sleep came and wrapped the whole body in love.

Dear Self:

As I look at my features in the mirror;
My own eyes had lost its shine, its glimmer;
the things that was seen from a child;
observed I as it burns in the pupil from life
moments full of crazy & wild.

The lips full with pucker;
To bravely open my mouth to punk out a coward
into a sucker;
As it went through punches to kisses;
To regain my word those were gains & full of misses.

My hands were full of blood from the piercing knife;
To regain my strength those were full of struggle and strife;
To holding & welcoming into the world a brand new life;
Wondering if I would ever hold hands & become some
man's wife.

My thighs were violated by a creep;
the truth about my past were oozing, it seeps;
To make love to strangers & my best friend in between
the sheets;
Oh the secrets-it keeps;
To wrestle with the blankets on learning how to sleep.

My feet have walked for miles until it sores;
To getting my ankles sprain, my foot gorges;
To feel life a woman, I do my own pedicure;
To keep it scraped, buffed and lotioned for the world;
To walk barefoot and free galore.

My body went through the pain;
Is there anybody to blame;
to be tortured, beaten & violated;
To go through the celebrations which it made
me elated;
It's great to be alive the body I have;
To protect my arms, legs, hands, and thighs this made it
to be saved

Anyways, until next time.....
My body will always be safe & fine.

I'm fed up with me, analyzing why me abuser(s) love to strike me in my face. When I was 14 yrs of age a male around the same age as I, at that time, punched me in my face which caused me to have a black eye. My brothers and myself wanted revenge, how dare he, to this very day I don't know why he punched me in my face, I'm now 51 yrs of age. At age 30 or there about I was punched in my face by my daughters father, he broke my nose and both eyes were blue black green and purple for nearly 6-8 wks. I felt as though I was total scum felt that people were always staring and talking about why I was wearing make-up in 100 degree weather, which is uncommon for myself. I vowed that my face is sacred territory felt violated humiliated. Three years later he swung a golf club at my face I managed to lean backward to avoid to golf club impact, I was in awe, shocked trembling trying to analyze why instead of packing up my belongings and grabbing our daughter and getting the hell out of

over

89

dodge. I later on left all together 6 months later, I was finally free, of that abusive relationship. At age 49 yrs I was punched in my face again, at age 51 I was punched in my face again, no more. I'm too beautiful to get punched hit, slapped, pushed on, any parts of my body. I'm a human being put here on earth for humanitarian purposes, I'm not going to tolerate any more barbaric tactics of any sort, this is not Gods purpose for mankind whatsoever. I've learned so much about me within this past year. I'm beautiful and need to be treated as such.

Dear cheeks,

I'm not sure which one of you got slapped more, but I'd like to apologize for never protecting either of you. I would like to blame it on my mother for not protecting us from him, but I knew that 9-1-1 was the only thing I had to dial in order to keep you from turning dark red and stinging. Did it hurt? I'm sorry. It wasn't your fault. It never was. Was it my fault? For years I believed that I deserved every slap, every kick, every push to the ground, every drop of saliva that landed right on my face... But I didn't. We were both victims of his rage that was set off by silly things. While other kids got grounded, we got a solid twenty minutes of full force swings, topped off with being trapped inside our room... subject to his anger for the next few days. I know it hurt, but the salty tears that slid off of you soothed the pain and soothed my soul.

As we grew up, I tried to win your love back with food, glorious food. You've tasted plenty of things and I'm sure you liked them all... The sweets that melted beneath my tongue, the salty chips that would leave a slightly disgusting yet still delicious after tase in our mouth. Even now, as I reflect on our hard times together, I'm giving you some yummy rocky road ice cream. I hope that it chills the stinging feeling that you used to feel. Luckily, I've learned to please you with healthy foods too. I'm glad we've come to terms on that, because my desire to please you jeopardized my health for a few years. Thank you for agreeing to like apples and bananas as much as you like M&Ms and french fries.

Cheeks, we're now 18 and that means that no one can ever hurt us again. The only way you will be touched is with my permission, and I promise you that the only way you will ever be touched from now on is with love. Do you remember the first time I let someone touch you with love? It was March 15th, 2013, only a few months ago. His thumbs stroked you with tender care. It felt unreal. It made the salty tears come back, but this time you were happy. Do you remember when he kissed you? Did you feel the smile I had? You must have, because you both felt my muscles pulling you upwards.

I'm sorry for what we had to deal with as children. But I promise that the only thing that you will ever feel again are fingers that caress you, kisses that make us smile, facial wash that takes care of you, and tears that soothe you.

All of my love,

Dearest Hands,

I applaud you. You have been a touchstone and conductor throughout my life. As a young child, you were my barometer of safe possibility, monitoring hot-and-cold, sharp-or-dull, steadying the step-stool, breaking my fall from a hop-scotch tumble. You taught me to hold and be held, to wave in eager greetings and wistful goodbyes. You trusted the many hands that held you as we crossed the city streets, and you were always the first hand raised in any classroom, undaunted by the possibility of a wrong response. Your innocence and curiosity were an invitation to imagination, and your dexterity often exceeded our tender years.

When I was three, you surprised me with your skillful affinity for ravioli-making, a day-long adventure involving three generations of Italian women wrapped in flour-sack aprons, grinding, rolling, and cutting out those scrumptious little cubes. You worked with such precision and intent…carefully filling the grinder with bits of meat and home-grown vegetables, focused and serious as you drove that ravioli cutter through rows and rows of doughy pasta squares… Ravioli-making was the precursor to music-making, and in the tradition of many Italian families I was eventually expected to set you to the task of accordion playing. My mother and grandfather were both accomplished players; their accordions were imported, handmade instruments exquisitely embellished with mother-of-pearl…their glittery names engraved in shiny rhinestones. We were mesmerized as their nimble fingers flew across the keys, and we swayed along the sidelines, clapping and tapping in time.

When our turn finally came to play you were so excited…anxious…ready to join the band. We had only three lessons in a stuffy windowless room above the dime store before the music teacher slapped you with a songbook and declared you unteachable…untalented and unworthy of participation in such a sanctified tradition. You dangled at my side in shame, wondering why you could not make those keys and buttons sing. Disgrace would have overtaken us had it not been for the intervention of my grandmother, a devout seamstress and meticulous mender of rips and tears. She neatly swept away our accordion aspirations and lovingly replaced them with a nine point quilter's needle and a spool of mercerized cotton thread; it was clear from the beginning, you were made to sew and cut against the grain. I quickly became the Queen of invisible stitching, hand-basting and frivolous appliqué. Together we fabricated the perfect textile niche, and I honestly believed that we had rebounded into redemption from our shame-filled musical debut.

But that redemption did not exempt us from calamity, and our proclivity for artistic stitchery made us no less vulnerable to seduction. That is why I cannot blame you for accepting the Bit-o-'Honey bar from the man who became our molester. You held yourselves out in innocent friendship and you were clasped in a vice grip of salacious behavior. You did not know that the secrets he asked you to hold were unspeakable and indelible. You did not understand the game of seduction or the power of silence as you covered my eyes and blinded me from the betrayal. You had no way to know how much that betrayal would shape my life. You could not foresee the crazy patchwork of battered self worth and rabid self doubt that would shroud us for many years to come.

And so, gradually we became artless, lost, grasping at anything that would blunt feeling. The affinities we once celebrated were now rarely summoned; I became a dabbler in self expression and a mistress of self reproach. Estranged from symmetry and design, we surrendered to numbness. Eventually we found solace wrapped around the shapely neck of a bottle of Jack Daniels Sour Mash, clutching it like a true friend and confidante. You learned to thump that glassy jigger softly on the bar and throw those straight shots back with wild conviction, gesturing to the bar men in trauma code...look, look at me... as I touch my face, smooth my hair and crook a flirty finger in your direction...And it was one of those burly bar men that finally handed us the romance we imagined we deserved.

They called him Billy-Rock because he once fell through a set of bleachers at a high school football game, and the only thing visibly broken was the bench. He appeared to be rock-solid...but we came to know his broken parts quite well. He hid them in a bottle of Tanqueray accessorized with a twist of lime and a frothy Guinness chaser. In the beginning, he held us tightly, kissed us gently and promised to cherish us forever. He sang like a fucking bird, and I was a sucker for a song. A few crooned bars of Brown-eyed Girl and I positively melted. And I thought I melted him too with my sassy San Francisco mystique and handy bohemian charm. I thought that right up until the first time he laid his meat-hook hands on me in anger.

I don't even remember why he did it. I never saw it coming. He shoved me hard against the wall and pinned us with his grip. I minimized it, excused it, came up with a million reasons why we shouldn't just wave goodbye. And when the shoves became grabs and the grabs became slaps and the slaps became fists, it never occurred to me that I was being battered; we simply cowered down and surrendered without resistance because we thought it was our fault. It had to be something in me that was triggering this in him, and if I could change it, then I could stop it…stop lying, stop isolating, stop hiding my bruises and my shame…then maybe he wouldn't hit me anymore and we could go back to the business of modern romance. You became deflectors of the blows, unable to initiate anything more than a silent plea to stop. We had to change something, and whether it was collusion or desperation, carelessness or destiny, ten months later our beautiful baby girl was born and that changed everything.

You held her like a doll-baby, a tiny little bundle of strange and mysterious joy. She was barely six months old the night Billy Rock staggered in from the Lone Star Bar reeking of Tanqueray and Tabu. I heard him stumble into the baby's crib and let out a stream of angry curses. I squeezed my eyes tighter and you yanked the blankets up over my head, praying she wouldn't wake up…that he would just fall into bed and leave us all alone. But he didn't. He flicked on the light, snatched me from the bed and began throwing me against the walls. I thought he was going to kill me; I envisioned my skull cracking wide open and my bloody brains splattering all over the shiny latex paint. He was yelling; you were flailing and I was begging him to stop, terrified that the baby would wake up and he would turn on her, my beautiful Brown-eyed Girl.

And then it stopped. Suddenly he just ran out of hate and anger and blows and crumpled to the floor. Within minutes he was snoring and snorting, oblivious to me and the mayhem he created. We passed him on our way to the kitchen, splayed out on the carpet like a beached whale, an easy mark. You knew exactly what to do. He didn't hear a thing as you pulled open the drawer and calmly selected the longest, sharpest knife among the chaos of salad forks and spatulas. You clutched the knife tightly as I knelt down beside his unsuspecting frame and contemplated where to stick the blade. On that night, in that room, holding that knife aimed and steady there was no doubt in my mind that I would kill him. None. That mother-fucker was never going to lay another hand on me in anger ever again. He would never have the opportunity to do to our daughter what he so freely did to me. Simple, clean, one deep two-handed thrust of the blade and that would be the end…no more fear and no more pain. You wrapped yourself around that smooth wooden handle and prepared us for glorious liberation.

That's when I heard the baby crying. She was probably crying all along, but I never heard it. It was only in that moment of lucidity, just before deliverance that I was clear enough to hear her frightened cries. And with those cries came another thought, "And then what? What will happen to this child if you plant this knife in this man's heart? Who will believe you? What will become of the life you created if you sacrifice your life for his death?" And just like that you dropped the knife, scooped up the bawling baby and walked over to the phone. You punched in the number for Suicide Prevention (only because there is no Murder Prevention number) and whoever it was on the other end of that phone talked us out of manslaughter. I would not add murder to my list of endless sins, not that night.

Instead, we traded the blade for a nine point quilting needle, and we began to sew. At first we quilted timidly, in isolation, meticulously applying the minutiae of instruction. Every pattern we attempted was safely outlined with preconceived dimensions, designated fabrics and suggested color schemes. My desire to create was alive, but my confidence and courage were hidden in the folds of personal trauma; color and whimsy were muted and elusive to my hand. Our creations were impeccably crafted, but often they were joyless replications in which no spirit or hint of me was evident. But you would not allow this to continue. You began inching toward raucous color and inspired design…tossing aside directions and replacing them with risky innovation. My artistic spirit was joyfully uncapped, and the patterns of creation literally bolted from our fingers to the cloth. The first piece I sold was entitled Cow Crazy, and it brought just enough cash for a one-way ticket to anywhere for Billy Rock and his Traveling Tanqueray Circus of Pain.

Many quilts have come and gone since then, some sold, many gifted, a handful traded to kindred creative souls. The needle may have been my salvation, but I still have the knife, still jumbled up in a chaotic kitchen drawer. I never use it, but I pull it out and look at it sometimes, sometimes to remember and sometimes to forget…the handle is scarred, the blade shaded and dull, and when you wrap your fingers around it, I remember how close I came to madness and how precious are the shaky hands of hope. Because of you dear hands, your deft application and fearless resolve, raviolis will be forever tasty; accordions do not rule the world, and dime-store cloth can miraculously reshuffle the remnants of a prefabricated life. I adore you…I revere you…I applaud your spunky essence and your tender, touching suture of the wound.

Dear vagina,

I don't understand you. Our first time you wanted so badly, the rush of pain was excrutiating, you froze and it felt as if our lover was trying to tear you apart. The pain was so bad, it took months before our lover could bear to finally press his way in. It didn't matter how much I trusted him...you resisted. Our brain insisted that something that it locked away from my mind was happening again. Terror. You clenching. Pain. I was only sixteen. I didn't know to do research, get help, reach out.

January first. The clock had just changed. The last thing I did in December was kiss him and it was the first thing I did in this new year. Finally you relaxed enough that I was able to convince him to go ahead and after a few minutes, I was able to convince you to finally trust him too. Our brain still warned you with each advance but now you could be pursuaded. I felt relief and without anyone to turn to, I assumed all girls must have this issue.

Fast forward six months. I sit, detached, as I am told that you were assulted. I beg for more information and am turned away. I seek out others who have the answers. They, too, turn me away. Who? What? When? How long? You can't tell me. They won't tell me.

Time passes. Brief intervals of pain are what you give me whenever I seek that physical attachment. I still know nothing of why you must act this way. He leaves and someone new takes his place.

At first we feel safe. You only provide me with the same pain. I think you are yelling to me, "Wait! I'm afraid!" but I don't speak vagina or we'd have a lot more figured out by now.

As the months go by you become more afraid. The pain becomes unbareable each time and I avoid sex like the plague even when I want it. This new lover has no patience for you. He doesn't care that you're afraid and even as I try to show him how to set you more at ease he forgets. He begs for you but refuses to register you're not like other vaginas. Places and spots that bring others pleasure is painful and you are sensative. Holding you open stretches still-tender scar tissue and each starting touch needs to be tender...gentle. I can't do this to you anymore. I satisfy him infrequently with hands and mouth all the while thinking, "What's wrong with me?"

I begin to search for answers. Honeymooners syndrome explains your symptoms and I move through the motions to fix your disdain of him but the information never sticks and I don't even want to try anymore and you're screaming to stop and inside I'm screaming.

What's wrong with me?

I fear sleep. The only time I sleep is when I sleep with Moon near me. Other times I pass out from exhaustion. I wake up naked from the waist down. I question him and he says I must have done it myself in my sleep. I don't sleep walk and this has never happened before. What's wrong with me?

He wants sex. Finally I agree to a threesome. They're drunk and they stumble through it. I let them and as I get pulled in it is nothing but pain. He is pain to you. She is pain to you. But I feel nothing. Eventually I sneak away to give you the release you need. You are sore, aching.

More months pass. I become closer to Moon. Though I am still tied to him I tryst. With Moon a second of pain is flooded by pleasure. A gasp or cry of pain and the motions stop and new ones begin. Even you plead for more. Your pain is momentary, brief and I feel normal again. I want again.

So I left him, Vagina. I still wish I could understand you. I wish someone would tell me who, what, when and how. You were hurt badly enough for stitches and I was given antibiotics on your behalf. They will never tell me what happened to you. But I know you could, if you'd only write back.

Love, me

Clavicle-
You're my axis
My point of symmetry
My frame
A gravitational pull
Keeping all my other bits and pieces at center

to my 1st boyfriend
You were handle bars
Carved by Seraphs neither of us believed in--

That was the 1st time I let someone else steer you...

Clavicle--
Two weeks ago
I lost you again
You became small
Shrunken
Beneath his hands--
Wobbly butterfly wings
RetRACting and unfurling
Gasping and undone
You held the tension
Of a thousand disquieted "no"s
Like pulses
Lifelines
The beating of tiny wings

Against a sweeping tide

Clavicle--
You are the oars
Of the boat he took me out on that night--
Submerged and resistant

Resisting

Resisting

A volition which is not your own

Baby Teeth,

Starting with my mother, who kept you in nightstands
Under layers of birthday cards, receipts, and fingerprint stained glasses
Teeth from the times I ate those apples after apples
Two from the time we punched you out to learn to whistle
Each of them placed under pillows, and sealed with unwanted kisses

I said to mother--you hide pieces of my nights.
Looking into her nightstand, there's evidence of bodies that never were
     whole
Children that had never known what it meant to have these baby-teeth
Each and all teeth shed served as evidence of he who abused his duties
     as the tooth-fairy

Once upon a time, we sat around the dinner table
Face closed and buried into plates of chicken and corn and rice
Mouth was too closed to eat
Didn't have any teeth left

There was a flash on Fox News: The story of Melissa Russell, her
30 seconds of fame muffled by the sound of my step-father's chewing-
     chew-chewed meat and scraping of hungry forks; her
30 second sound bite made no mention childhood fits neatly into
     drawers
30 seconds forgot that quarters her tooth-fairy left under her pillow will
     never buy back what she has lost.

That's when he asked me, "Do you know what rape is?"
Mother slid on those finger-print stained glasses, leaving me and him
Alone
     1. We were nose to nose
     2. We were fingerprint to fingerprint
     3. We were eye to eye
     4. We were eye to fingerprint
     5. We were mouth to fingerprint
     6. We were mouth to mouth
     7. We were mouth to chest
     8. We were mouth to cunt
Repeat

What is rape?
9 year old me had not known what it meant to have every baby-tooth
      stolen-swollen shut
She did not know, had never known
But her body did

Cover that in 30-second news clips
Cover me under covers of birthday cards, receipts
Under layers, celebrity gossip and Tuesday's traffic report
How can you cover a life in 30 seconds when I didn't even have
30 seconds to say no

Dear Lips:

You are so courageous;
To speak against a coward so fearless;

To speak boldly about the truth;
when others do not want to confront;

From wanted to passionately being kissed;
From a stranger to my best friend who I truly missed;

To apply red lipstick to look good and being a conservative Christian;
To pray and speak to a true god to whom I trust in;

Continue speaking up lips with true bravery;
Without speaking is like being shackled in a abuse slavery;

You cannot shut this lip up;
I have so much to say that will make my enemy stomped;

So keep on talking my brave lips;
To keep on proven cowards wrong by their actions they continue to slip;

Keep pressing forward without any intimidation;
Continue to express yourself through creation.

Anyways until next time.......

Dear V,

Though you have been part of me since birth, I have not loved you as I should have when others hurt you. I said nothing, did nothing and devalued your ability to produce joy. I was unable to keep you safe, but this was not reason enough to deny your purpose.

Before you were given a chance to blossom, I allowed you to be frozen in time. Feeling was passed off to mind and filtered into the beyond. Beyond sight and sound I found a safer place for you. Hidden in thought, you journeyed far away from the possibility of pain. Why have I not yet retrieved this most important part of you? Is it not now safe? Do I not now know what a blessing you could be, if once again whole? Why do I yet hesitate?

There have been moments, bubbles in time, where I have granted access to fulfillment. Even so, on your own, you learned to produce extra lubrication to protect yourself. This skill of survival misrepresents any connection to touch. Thoughts flood the mind and work their way back to you, beckoning you to escape when there is no danger. How can I now convince you to stay?

I picked out a bumper sticker for my VW Beetle announcing to the world my love for you. This overture did not convince you to stay. Time and again, you continue to run away.After nearly four decades on the lamb, I feel the need to apologize. I'm so very sorry that I did not value your worth. You are more than a womb and thank you for hosting life to three. You are more than warm tissue disposing of unfertilized eggs. You are fearfully and wonderfully made. You have the capacity to recreate the aurora borealis across the expanse of the nerve endings deep inside.

Once again, I plead with you; stay. It is now safe. I do love you and cherish your part in the function of living. We can do more than survive this existence. I will not ask you to flee again. I set you free.

Forever & Always,

To my eyes,
My beautiful eyes:

Do not feel as though you betrayed me, like you should have somehow said "no," but actually, accidentally, said "yes." You shouldn't have said anything, because you're eyes, and you can't speak, at least not like all those bullshit stories you've read would have you believe. I know sometimes you feel like you should have done a better job trying to show your fear, or maybe like you should have jumped out of my head and screamed, "STOP!" But you didn't, couldn't, and I don't blame you for it. I blame his eyes for seeing only my body, and his brain for thinking only about his. I blame his heart for not feeling at all, and his hands for feeling too much. I blame every part of his body that violated me, but no part of my body for being violated. My eyes, you used to sparkle with happiness, like the sun on a clear, blue sea, but this cloud has loomed over you for far too long, rained too many tears on pale cheeks. Weep no more because of him. What happened can't be changed, but we can take comfort in the fact that he will never rape or assault me ever again. Although he will never be tried for his crimes, I left him, and he can no longer harm me. My eyes, I say again that I neither blame you, nor myself. But I beg of you, my eyes, please forgive me for making you look at him for those two long years.

Love always,

3RD EYE
You know that I know,
You told me so.
You prod and you preen,
You purify the in-between.
The knowing, the seeing, the being.
You connect my dots from here to there.
From here to there is now.
Now is yesterday and now is tomorrow.
Remembering and foreseeing;
One a constant, the other a constant variable.
You remind that the hinge, the variable, is now.
What do I do now?
Who am I now?
You know that I know,
You told me so.
Earth to heaven, heaven to earth;
The knowing, the seeing, the being.

To the abused abusers in our chests,
For it is you though it is me.
To play with a mind is to slap in the face—the monsters we are provoked the monsters within. He claimed innocence in your moves but you knew every step. Knowing they were breaking. knowing I was in agonizing pain, all he did was make us worse. But I returned the favour. If he is at fault, we are just as much.
I wish I could forget it all. I wish I could forgive it all. But there was no ending justice. There was no saving grace. I ran away, looking back only to see mockery. I can't say I still feel but I also can't see the face or I may. Nor hear the name. Nor think of the way we danced; that is, when we did not brawl. O, my open wounds. If looks could kill, those bedroom eyes would have us dead. You, little heart, have love so boundless but only given where it was not. Dragging me down such rocky roads only to arrive in a desert alone… I couldn't understand it. I couldn't handle my frustration that was inside of you.
I just wanted him, the heartless, to hurt:
We kicked each other in the chest,
I cannot bear to wish you the best.

To my dearest Face

I do apologise if addressing you like this makes you feel somehow separate from the rest of the body. Your behaviour and role in my life has already cast you in that mould. I am extremely grateful for this. You were already protecting the inner layers before my first memories. All the negative emotions were always suppressed and perfectly well hidden. You managed so well to keep doing what you had to do no matter what was going on underneath. Your cover was always perfect.

When my sister was born, I was disappointed that she would never be "normal". The doctors were not able to untangle the cord from around her neck quickly enough to prevent permanent brain damage. Everybody was so worried about her. All the adults were too busy comforting my parents and trying to find cures and praying and so many other things that were more important than me. I didn't know how to say that I was also sad. There was nobody to talk to about how I felt cheated. All my cousins had siblings they could play with. Mine would never be able to walk or talk. It was so unfair. You understood that this would just give my parents something else to worry about when they had so much to deal with already. You knew that I had to be the easy child to make it easier for everybody to cope with this crisis.

Instead of showing the disappointment, you turned it around and made sure everyone knew that I was going to become a brain surgeon so that I could help to heal people. This is the first mask I remember wearing.

Even when I was 7 I had a way with words. It probably had something to do with my Dad taking me to the library every Saturday of our lives. That also meant that I spoke more eloquently than most kids my age. One of my teachers decided that it would be a good idea for me to speak at a school assembly. I was so nervous I thought I was going to wet my pants. Instead of giving in to that fear, you pulled us through it beautifully. You understood that one didn't disobey one's elders, especially not a teacher. You knew that it was an honour to be asked and that it would make my parents proud.

You showed no hint of the terror beneath the surface. Everyone thought I was the cutest little thing on the planet. There started the reputation for being a big mouth, so brave and outspoken. It was the perfect persona to hide the frightened little girl within. Suddenly I was an extrovert. I was on the inter house debate team, played sport, talked back to teachers… and still got decent marks all through primary school without even trying. The longer I wore this mask the more real it felt. It became a habit to never show any doubts or fears or pain.

When my sister died I went through all kinds of inner turmoil. While she was coughing up blood by the bucketful, I was praying harder than I had ever prayed in my 13yrs of being brainwashed into believing in the Pantheon of Hindu deities and the Christian God. None of them saved my sister from dying. I lost my faith in all Gods and Goddesses in the moment the doctor said, "I'm sorry. It's too late". My sister's death was therefore a double blow. It was the loss of a sibling without the comfort of religion. This was on top of all the emotional and developmental crap of becoming a teenager.

Everybody told me to be strong. They couldn't stop telling me how hard it was for my parents. I didn't need to be told. I had seen my father cry for the first time ever when he started making phone calls to the family to let them know. I couldn't add to that pain by showing mine. I couldn't let them see how much they needed to worry about me. You came to the rescue yet again.

Instead of showing the hurt and the pain and the confusion, you kept it together beautifully. You made sure people went away talking about how strong I was, how well I was handling this. When my parents sent me to the school guidance counsellor, who was the closest thing to a psychologist that we had, you took over so amazingly well. You told him all the normal healthy things that he wanted to hear. After just one session he was convinced that we were fine. He believed that the fact that we couldn't talk about it meant that we were strong and handling everything well. You even managed to go through all the rituals and sing all the hymns without weeping and wailing in absolute torment at the pointlessness of it all. You kept this facade going for years. Playing the right roles through Hindu service at home on Thursdays and even going to church with friends and extended family on Sundays. You showed me to be the perfectly dutiful daughter.

The schizophrenia was starting to take its toll. Later that same year the suicide attempts started. I just couldn't keep going. I wanted to die. That was it. I just couldn't live with this duality anymore. I took some of my mom's blood pressure medication. I left just enough tablets for her to have a dose that night and one the next morning. My body had a survival instinct. I started throwing up. After much questioning I finally admitted what I had done. My mom, being a nurse, knew how to handle the physical effects. She made me drink very strong salt water to throw up all the toxins. I slept for a long time after that. When I woke up you took over again.

Instead of trying to explain all the pain and suffering and hidden emotions that had no words, you told them that I wanted to be with my sister. You told them that I thought if I died too I would see her again and be able to tell her that I loved her. You showed no hint of disappointment when they decided that it was all okay. You nodded and agreed not to talk about it again. You accepted that it was more important to avoid the stigma of mental instability than to deal with the reality of the pain and suffering that was going on under the surface. I didn't. While you were saying all the right words and being suitably contrite and apologetic, my tortured soul within was screaming out for help. Yet somehow, the masks always won. The need to keep up appearances was always stronger than the need to get help.

For the next few years these separate realities continued to co-exist. For months at a time everything would be fine. I would keep the inner turmoil under check and you would continue to show the strong confident go getter personality. You would answer politely when everyone asked you which university you were going to attend and what you wanted to study. You never once let me scream out in rage about the lack of choice. You never once dropped the mask and said that what I really wanted was a break from the stress of academic bullshit. It all built up so that in the middle of all the normality, without warning I would suddenly take an overdose of whatever I could lay my hands on for no apparent reason.

Eventually, half way through matric my parents finally gave up the pretence that I was normal and checked me into a mental institution. The only good that came of it was that I started smoking consistently. I had tried a few times before but sort of on and off at parties every now and then. In the loony bin I learned to use it as a coping mechanism. I knew that it was bad for my health. My Dad had had 3 heart attacks by then and the first thing all the doctors agreed about was that he should stop smoking and drinking.

You even managed to hide this for a couple of years. I guess it also had a lot to do with Mum believing what she wanted to believe. Her clever, beautiful angel couldn't possibly be stupid enough to smoke. Knowing that I was killing myself slowly and gradually meant that the sudden attempts at suicide became less frequent.

Then Dad died. You managed to keep it together at the funeral. My most distinct memory of that day is going into the bathroom to cry. You had done such a good job over the years of maintaining the facade of strength and control, I just couldn't ruin it all by doing something as weak as crying in public, not even at my Dad's funeral. That girl is just amazing. Look at what life has thrown at her and she just takes it in her stride. She is so strong, so positive. She is her father's daughter.

Then I became even more my father's daughter. The drinking and the smoking got completely out of control. Even you couldn't save my reputation. I was partying with the boys because very few girls were allowed to party in public the way I did. I thought I was one of the guys. The guys that knew me well knew better than to treat me like a girl. You made sure of that. You wore that right masks to put us in the friend zone. Unfortunately everything has a limit. Eventually there had to be a guy that treated me like a girl – a girl who drank and smoked and partied like a boy, which meant that she had to be promiscuous as well. He raped me. It wasn't because he was some kind of monster. It was because he genuinely couldn't comprehend that a girl who behaved like I did was not only a virgin but also actually didn't want to have sex with him. He truly believed that I was playing hard to get. No matter how hard we fought he just couldn't break free of his rape culture conditioning to understand what we were telling him. For the first time in a long time you and I were saying the same thing together very loudly but it didn't help anything. We couldn't stop what was happening.

While I was dying on the inside you took control again. You didn't let any trace of the inner turmoil surface. There was no point in reporting it. Even you couldn't pull that off. Yes officer I had been drinking with boys who were not even related to me. Yes officer I was in the back seat of his car. He didn't stop when I asked him to and tried to push him off. That is officially rape. You and I were in agreement again. That was not an option.

So we went back to what worked. I was dying on the inside and you made sure nobody knew it. We went on as if nothing had happened. I drank more. I smoked more. I tried drugs but it didn't work for me. I failed 3 out of 4 courses at university. Mother dearest refused to continue paying for me to party so I went out and got a job.

Then I spent 6 months in Israel. Wow. I could be anyone I wanted to be. Nobody knew me. Nobody had any expectations. Nobody really cared. All the volunteers were there to party. All the kibbutzniks knew this. Nobody judged the girls who partied as hard as the boys. I was saved from the sleeping around part of the partying by a beautiful gay boy. For some reason he felt safe confiding in me and asked me to pretend to be his girlfriend so he wouldn't be harassed by all the macho soldier types.

This suited me perfectly. I was still afraid of the whole sex scene. Since he was honest with me, I returned the favour. We told him about the rape. You and I were expressing things together again. Your clarity combined with my need to let out some of the crap. The relationship with the gay boy (who shall remain nameless to protect the beauty of what we shared) was perfect. It was wonderful emotional bonding, complete honesty and no sex. What more could a girl ask for?

That worked really well, until my 21st birthday. Gay boy took me to lunch in Tel Aviv. We started drinking red wine at about 11am. We got back to the kibbutz in time for dinner with one of the young soldier girls. Dinner was accompanied by cheap vodka. It turned out that dinner was a well-planned distraction to keep me out of the volunteer area while everyone arranged my real party. One of the other South Africans made me a special birthday "down -down". It was every type of alcohol they could lay their hands on in a mug with just enough cola to disguise the taste. I had to down it in one go. Needless to say by the time we got to the pub at the neighbouring kibbutz I was completely sozzled. My memories of that night are very vague with lots of gaps.

I was told that I had disappeared a few times so even gay boy couldn't paint a full picture. All I know is I woke up in my own bed in my undies, alone. The next night a really hot guy from the other kibbutz came over to take me out for pizza and ice cream. Gay boy and I had been drooling over him for almost a month since he kissed us both on the lips at the New Year's Eve party. Apparently in my drunken state the previous night I had agreed to go out with him, not that I would have refused if I had been sober. I just didn't remember. Gay boy and I "broke up" the next day. Everyone was amazed by how we managed to remain such good friends.

The boy next door (I think it's safe to call him Itzik – it's quite a common Israeli name) and I got very close very quickly. That's when you and I went our separate ways again. I couldn't let him know how scared and insecure and inexperienced I was when it came to physical relationships. I just didn't know how to talk to him about stuff like that and neither did you. He must have figured it out somehow. Lots of other volunteers were having sex and talking about it quite openly. I just couldn't.

Even though we knew our time together was limited, he was very patient and respectful. He was soft and gentle and always stopped as soon as I asked. One night the effort he put into creating the perfect romantic atmosphere finally overcame my fear. It was everything we are conditioned to expect of our first time (except for the being married bit and the fact that it wasn't my first time).

He had somehow managed to get keys to an empty volunteer room on our kibbutz. He had cleared away the furniture leaving only some mattresses on the floor. There were candles all around the mattresses with a few plates of snacks and a bottle of wine close by. You and I were one again. There was no faking anything. It was the most beautiful experience of my life up to that point (only surpassed by my husband many years later). I even cried in his arms afterwards. He just held me and let me weep until I was done. He didn't ask for any explanations and I didn't offer any. It was what it was and it was perfect. You took over again and protected that memory. While I cherished the experience, you played it out as part of the party girl image. As far as everyone else (except gay boy) was concerned, it was just a normal volunteer – kibbutzniks fling. There was always the awareness that it was a temporary physical relationship. Nobody else ever got to see the true depth of what it meant to me. You made sure everyone, including Itzik, knew that it was just a game.

Then I had to come home again. The cultural shock of returning to the closed Indian community of Durban in post-election South Africa turned me nearly schizophrenic. I think that was the point at which you got your own separate personality. For a time I even called you Denise. We went back to not smoking in public or in front of our elders but the partying took on a new spin. I was looking for the physical bonding again. Because part of the magic had been the understanding that it was temporary and mostly physical, I went through a ridiculous number of one night stands and purely physical relationships.

I knew what I was looking for and my heart ached at the emptiness of what I found instead and yet I had to keep looking. Somebody had to realize that it wasn't just about taking advantage of a slut. I just ended up feeling cheap and abused every time. I was lonely and hurting and it felt like nobody could possibly understand what I was going through so I didn't bother to talk to anyone. You kept it all in line. You made my slut phase appear to be fun. You created the reputation of being able to walk into a pub and choose who I would sleep with that night. You created the party girl image and revelled in it. You turned the bad reputation into a feminist statement. You stood up to people for whom you were supposed to play the good girl regardless of the talking behind your back. On the inside I didn't know whether to laugh or cry at the illusion of honesty.

Mom couldn't deal with the way I was living my life and gave me the, "as long as you live under my roof" speech. I chose to not live under her roof and moved into my own place. You and I became even more detached. The more I died on the inside the more you became the life of the party. The more confidence you threw out there the less confident I felt on the inside.

Around this time I met Costa, the man who would become my husband. You played the games and tried to keep me safe by pushing him away when he got too close. I was so wrecked on the inside. I hated the schizophrenia. I hated feeling so fake all the time. I hated not knowing where I ended and where you began. I hated everything about myself so much that I couldn't see how anybody could love me.

Costa has spent the last 17 years trying to help me see things differently. There have been many times when you and I have been able to join forces to communicate with him together. He is the person who has allowed us to be most real. He is the main reason we have reached a point where we are almost one again.

With him we have had 2 beautiful children. From the safety of his love we have discovered our own beauty and strength. This has allowed us to be real with more people. We have been able to find true friendships and build honest relationships.

There are times when you still need to protect me. Sometimes it is even still with Costa (no relationship is perfect and we do disagree about some things and have had our fair share of screaming matches) or the children or with friends. Sometimes when dealing with strangers. Mostly though, it feels like we are becoming one completely.

Thank you for keeping me safe. I was taught very early in life that other people's opinions were more important than my truth. You allowed me to be what everybody wanted me to be on the outside while keeping my truth safe from the mockery of a society that couldn't understand my real needs. Sometimes it feels like most of my life up until very recently was just one long string of emotional neglect and abuse. Your ability to help me pretend otherwise is probably all that kept me relatively sane. Without your brave façade, I would have been completely alienated by my weirdness. There was a very definite limit to how far one was allowed to stray from the norm. Your ability to project what was necessary allowed me the internal freedom to explore all the subversive ideas that are now acceptable in the new family that I have found.

Thank you for letting me shine through when I needed to share my truth with people who deserve it. They have helped me to know that sibling rivalry is normal. Questioning religious dogma is not only acceptable but even desirable and a sign of higher intellect. Women have the right to choose whether to smoke, drink alcohol and have sex as much as they want to without being judged. I was not to blame for being raped. I am worthy of being loved. I deserve to speak my needs and have them met.

I love knowing that I can hide behind you or I can speak my truth through you. What I love most is that it is becoming a conscious choice rather than a knee jerk reaction.

I thank you and I love you, my face.

In unity forever

To My Beautiful Eyes:

My dearest eyes, what pain and suffering you have seen. Your deep blue rings are the crevasses that hold the whispers of your anguish. I am sorry I could not shield you from the realities of this world, this place. People are always paying you compliments. People always say that they have so much depth and are so dynamic; you truly are gorgeous. But the life you have illustrated is haunting. The steel blue iris provides a backdrop for the flecks of gold and silver that mark the scars of the hell you have seen and lived through. The navy blue ring that holds your deepest secrets in place is the same color as the midnight sky that you spent countless nights staring out into, hoping the pain would end. But within you my beautiful eyes, you also show a shade of hope. The sea green ribbons that are washed over your stenciled stories signify the crashing of the waves, and with every blink, the pain and the horrifying illustrations are taken back into the depths of the sea.

So my dearest beautiful eyes, thank you for being so serene and vibrant. Keep my story safe and provide me the new images of my future that you will shine so brightly for.

With pure devotion,

Ode to my Body Art!

Such beauty that decorates my skin! You transform me into something new! There may not be many of you, I don't have sleeves or complete coverage of my skin, but those of you that live on me speak volumes of who I am!

My Unicorn, you were my first tattoo. Don't let anyone tease you for being so feminine, you are a treasure! You rescued me during a pivotal moment in my teens. You ushered in adulthood for me. You told my mother that I did not belong to her anymore. You belted it out from the top of your lungs that the only scars that would don my body from that moment on would be works of art. You're simple design and black coloring fits the humble desire to live beyond my abusive mother while never forgetting the dark clouds that you emerged from. I chose you because of your beauty and the fantasy world you exist within. You led me across the bridge from the harsh and painful reality I used to reside within into the dream and hope for a life without abuse, a life of freedom! I'm indebted to you!

And then, there's my Phoenix. My proud, strong, fiery phoenix! You sit upon my shoulder, shouting to the world that you are born from the ashes of fire! You are entwined with vibrant hues of fire and smoke. You've risen from the scorching flames of rape and incest. You've been reborn stronger and more powerful than ever before. You carry no shame in your past. The shame belongs to my father, not to you, not to me. He alone is filled with the guilt of his heinous acts. I am no longer held back by the chains of fear and insecurity. I no longer carry around the stigma of being a victim. You, dear Phoenix, are my declaration that I am a survivor! I am proud to show you off. I am excited to share my story of survival with anyone who will listen. Phoenix, you offer many opportunities to share my story and express the hope I've discovered. The hope that life does go on, and it does get better!

And finally, there's my Puzzle. Oh you are so interesting! You look like someone cut out a piece of puzzle-shaped flesh, revealing a lake of fire under my skin. You continue my story. I mean really, no one's story is ever finished. You, Puzzle, express the Phoenix infiltrating my entire being. Parts of my body were desecrated by my father, but Puzzle you harmonize with Phoenix. You allow a glimpse of how the Phoenix has transformed my captivity into total freedom. Your shape, the puzzle piece, exhibits that I'm putting my life back together. After everything I've suffered by the hands of my father and my mother,

Puzzle, you show that I am a survivor. And I can put the pieces back into place, creating an incredible work of art out of the life I have been blessed with. Its fitting you reside on the top of my foot. My feet are the first to touch the path I walk each day. I don't ever want to forget how far I've come. You express the consumption of the Phoenix's principles from top to bottom.

Dear Tattoos, I am planning just one more work of art to celebrate my independence. You all harmonize so well in telling my story, I'm sure you'll welcome your new friend with open arms and great appreciation!

With Much Love,

Mind,

You've never written to a body part before, let alone really addressed yourself. You've been taught that talking to yourself is madness and madness is a social taboo. So you mainly stayed still, silent... or only talking in theoreticals and second person point of view.

Your mother always told you that children are to be seen and not heard. Your words are a noisy nuisance, she said. Your teachers told you that "I" is wrong and should never be written. Your experiences are invalid, they said. Your society told you that expressing your hurt, pain, rage, and helplessness shouldn't happen. Your feelings are too much for us to handle, they said, so they must be wrong. You were taught to keep it all in and let it turn and churn. No one ever taught you what to do when it all comes exploding out when no more thoughts can fit.

Your mother hated you and your capacity for independent thought. But more importantly, she hated herself and the life she chose. She took her hatred, confusion, and loneliness out on you, breaking you down with fatalistic threats, demeaning comments, and snippets of vitriol.

Those times where you were jarred inside your head after hearing her speak, well, her hand caused that. The times that you were so scared and confused and without guidance or comfort, her fear caused that. The neglect sunk in deep. The hits and words having not left lasting physical marks, but emotional ones. The marks your hands left on your own body have stayed much longer than hers.

The depression, the hoping every day that death will take you home is not your fault. For without ever having received nurturing, caring, guidance, an actual place to call home...

You'd have been brought to your knees so many times if you had them. You are a strong and resilient ever-present part of me. If it weren't for you I'd still be lost and alone.

I am telling you now with 27 years of experience that you matter. No matter what your mom, your society, or your own thoughts sometimes say. You and all the emotions and thoughts and words you produce are important. You can change the world with the love and wonder you have. They...well...

117

They never will.

Love,

My Dearest Heart,

What words could possibly express the sadness I feel when I think of how badly I trapped you. Encapsulated you. Hid you. Removed you. Denied your existence. (sigh)

I Held you prisoner behind stone walls, walls that eventually had to be chipped away by the angels, one tiny painful tap at a time.

How does one describe that ordeal? From one loving soul to another, I'm sure you understand the need for safety and protection, Yours, as well as my Own. You did, didn't you? Do you? Don't you? Understand that is?

Still, I can't imagine how it felt to be you. To be part and parcel of the journey, one with me, supporting me actually, yet left hidden, denied, closed off, unseen and unheard. But (in my mind) therefore, protected. Please understand the need. It was for Our protection, Mine as well as Yours. You get that don't you?

I imagine you must have felt so isolated and alone. The same way I did. And all the while, you were beating strong for me. Strong paddled heartbeats remaining constant while I, unnoticed, dallied with near syncope.

Can you ever forgive me?

Together, the journey has brought us to this place where we join hands (so to speak) and drum our rhythm together, understanding the cloak has been removed, the shelter unnecessary, the world not quite so fearful.

Now, I breathe you in not close you off. Now, I feel your love and send it outward.

Welcome back to me my loving friend.

Welcome home.

Your mind, heart, and spirit, woven
with the strength of three strands braided
for resiliance, which is the treasure
within you that has been attempted to
be claimed, suppressed, and used, in
thievery of what was never available
for approach to be taken, changed,
suppressed, or claimed, and you have
weathered the damages of many attempts,
staving off what was yours and always
will be.
    Life is breathed into existence with
life purpose - special purpose, passed
down through generations. Never let go
of who you are.

Love from,

After again always another around away back bed before body brain care days Dear
enough every everything eyes face fear feel felt finally first full
give good hands head heart held here hold hope hurt inside keep knew lay left life little
long look love made man many maybe mind months more Mother mouth myself need
never new night nothing now once over own pain part past real really remember right
room safe said see show skin sleep someone sometimes sorry still stop
strong take tell thought time times together told touch tried trying understand used
want words world years

These are the 100 most used words in the letters / these homes / these
places / these pieces that they tried / are trying so hard to keep safe.
The letters, words, and stories that survivors live. These are homes that
they make, these places that they store memories locked into bodies that
sometimes don't feel like theirs, these pieces that they pick up
    and move away with.

This book is for the times survival meant try-tried-trying to share a piece
of our body to others to hold, to carry, to say and feel that :

Even after you have been hurt again and again and always another time,
you can come around and away and never back to the bed and the body
and the brain broken from someone you thought cared; like days that
feel dear and dirty or when you had enough of every everything, like
your eyes and your face and your fear. Sometimes you still feel what you
felt when it felt final or like the first time or full of _____.

You can give. You have good hands, head, and heart that held on. Stay
here and hold hope when it hurts inside to keep what you knew when
you lay empty and left life for a little.

So long it took to look for love made with many patience for your
maybes and didn't mind waiting months more. So long it took for you to

find love from a Mother who has a mouth that cares as much for you as myself. Sometimes you need what you never knew, like a new night where nothing happened. Now, once, again, I want to tell you that I will never be over your own pain that others claim to only be part of your past. It's real—really real. Even if you can't remember everything right or if the room doesn't feel safe and you don't know why. You said as you drifted asleep, see show skin sleep someone sometimes sorry still stop.

You are strong for taking and telling: I thought every time you told of the times how hard it is to feel together or touched. You tried and are trying to survive when it is hard to understand how not to feel used.

You are worthy of so many wants and words and worlds.
You are worthy of a body that only you can use for years to come.

You are as strong as all of the bones between these pages.

Survival

Tips, tricks, and activities to make writing something heavy a release; a list compiled by the writers of *Portable Homes*.

Please note that not every suggestion on this list is a safe or viable option for every body

1. trace an outline of your body onto a large piece of paper; use it as a map to write in your stories and landscapes

2. call a friend who knows you through everything

3. write down all of your insides and then rip up the paper

4. dance with your eyes closed

5. make a list of all the people and places that make you feel safe; put the list somewhere where you will see it on a regular basis

6. pursue a new language, which carry new words that resonate

7. fill a room with holiday lights (at least four strands)

8. take photographs on days you are moving forward

9. Play with your cat
10. Make a map of how to get to your favorite place; include the process of getting ready to go there, who you will see on your way, what you are wearing, etc.

11. Write down all the lies you can remember being told about your body even if you still believe them (ESPECIALLY if you still believe them) and tear up the pages or burn them.

12. paint your hands and feet; leave prints of yourself in places that matter to you

13. this: thewildernessdowntown.com/

14. take bites out of paper before or after writing on it
15. make a video or audio recording of yourself reading your writing out loud

16. Spend time with people/in places that make you feel safe.

17. Finding something to climb

18. send mail to someone that you miss

19. Put your inner script to the test. If you think you're ugly, stand naked in front of a mirror and list what's wrong with your forehead, hair, cheeks, ears... All the way to your toes. You'll find there are parts of you that are beautiful, normal, healthy. If you think you are helpless, make a list of all that you do every day by yourself: you drive, you fix your food, you work...

20. Keep a gratitude journal in which you list 5 things you're grateful for, no matter how simple. The only rules are that you cannot list the same thing more than once a week without a specific reason and you must find 5 things every day. Over time, this helped me cultivate a spirit of optimism by teaching me to -expect- positivity in my everyday life.

21. Rearrange the furniture

22. Write out your thoughts then burn it. So when you are able to get your feelings out but feel better by releasing all your thoughts. Take deep breaths, talk it out then let it go.

23. Pray. Have a deep and a personal relationship to our heavenly father by praying intensely on things that are bothering you.

24. Keep yourself busy by doing nothing but positive things with yourself or people who has supported you through your darkest

moments. It has always help me with the support of my aunt (who has always been a mother to me), my cousin, my child, and the guidance from my heavenly father it has always keep me positive like watching comedy, listen to music, take a walk and etc.

25. Find a friend to sit back to back with--share your weight.

26. Learn how to roller skate to feel infinite.

Responses to:

Please write a little something about your experience in writing your piece(s) for *Portable Homes*

This has literally revealed new light and healing for my soul. I had no idea just how far I've come in my journey, not to mention how much further I still need to go. I have renewed love and respect for myself. My body is a work of art. It has an incredible story to tell, and I'm honored to get to share that story.
Andrea Van Winkle

I found writing for Portable Homes to be healing and feel more validated in having felt hurt and afraid.
Kye

I would have never guessed that simply acknowledging the worth of one body part would refocus my thought patterns so quickly. I edited my letters up to five times until the words flowed with proper intention and sentiment. In rereading the first few drafts of each, I could see clearly how my thought transitions pushed through the negative debris to find something pleasant and purposeful. Owning every part of oneself as equally as each facet of a gem lends possibility to polish oneself from the inside out with no fear to shine.
Betty Jean

Having been taught that being a victim was shameful, I find it quite empowering to be able to share our experiences in this manner.
Angie Ng

The experience gave me a sense of being part of a noble pursuit. A soaring deed that does not recoil against the blood that has been shed in the name of abuse prevention and suffering of any kind. It reminded me that the truth is more important than life itself. Without truth – there is no life. And the experience also reminded me that I am: a father, a writer, a survivor. That [we] must all struggle against the darkness.

Therefore, I leave this memory of my experience in your gentle and fierce hands. With love and hope to my dear friends this record that begins with ... when I was just a boy.
Gregg Tyler Milligan

I have grown a great deal from my experience. I have overcome the depression and the sadness that had smothered me for so long. I still have my days where it gets tough. But I know how to manage it now. I know how to put it away and function with my feelings and memories. That's how I have grown. I am no longer a victim. I don't feel like one. I have found a spriitual center where I can heal and kinow that I am loved. It has been a huge God send to me. I am grateful for this place. I can be me and no one judges me. We need more places like this in this world.
Amber Galey

How exhilirating and therapeutic it is to write and have someone listen....I didn't realize how much I was bursting at the seams to express myself! I used to take creative writing as a child, but this exercise seems so much more meaningful, especially in light of the traumatic events that have occurred in the years after my innocent youth...Thank you for this opportunity! I was inspired by Eve Ensler's "In the Body of the World".
Leia

I found when I looked at my body in a way that made me see every story that is attributed to it; I felt an overpowering sense of accomplishment. I feel a new sense of accomplishment because my story is what it is, because my body kept me safe throughout the journey of life so far.
Anonymous

I feel very lucky to have an opportunity to write a piece for this book. When people look at you as a "victim" (I prefer the word survivor) they automatically assume we are traumatized and leave it at that. They do not know how our opinions of ourselves, body and mind have changed. The battle is long, emotional and very confusing, but in the end it makes us stronger. Thank you so much for this opportunity to have our voices heard.
Ashlyn Lincoln

This has been the most awesome experience I ever had-this has given me a chance to use my talent to encourage any abuse survivor/victim that THERE is a life after abuse. It takes alot of empowerment, self-discovery, and faith to accept the things that had happened and forgive those who had tried everything to hurt me at its worse. All I can say is: "Never let these bullies (who can also be family members as well) shut your voice down. You are worth every fight for yourself."
Doris M. Jones

Even though writing is my main go-to coping mechanism for trauma, I had never written to myself or a part of my body before this project. My first instinct was to write to myself as a whole human being, one that thinks and feels and moves and lives, not as a person's hand, or stomach, or face. I felt an odd unease at writing to a part of my body, as if I weren't doing the rest of myself justice, as if I were leaving the other parts of me behind on the journey. I felt a sort of dehumanization and self-objectification that was confusing to me. I thought, "Is is detrimental for me to write to a part of myself? What does this mean to me? Should I do this if it seems so wrong?" I continued to think about my feelings for over a week, not putting words to paper or word document. It wasn't until I started getting regular updates from Attention: People With Body Parts through email and on Facebook that I really started questioning why it was so difficult for me to fathom how writing to one part of my body could be a positive. It was when someone's already-submitted poem was shared that I realized that if another survivor could do it, I could too. I sat down and tried to think of what part of my body had been assaulted and traumatized the most. Throughout the physical and mental abuse I've undergone, the oppression I had undergone psychologically from several people and situations was the most pervasive and tramatizing out of all the abuse. I wondered if the brain was a valid thing to write about. But my brain wasn't what was traumatized, really. Sure, I've had a concussion from being in a mosh pit or boxing, but never from abuse. My brain had never really been injured. So, I wondered if a mind was a tangible part of a body. My mind is what has been injured the most. I figured that I would write to my mind because without the functions of the rest of my body and my brain, my mind wouldn't exist. After deciding this, the words flowed. The dehumanization and objectification that I was worried about in the beginning vanished. I felt okay, which is a huge step up from feeling traumatized and upset. After writing, I reread my poem at least 10 times before submitting it. After a few changes over the

next couple days, I finally became completely comfortable and proud of my contribution. It is now something I'm proud to associate my name with.
M. Osborn

Honestly, I was hesitant to do this project. I was scared of where it would take my heart and mind, afraid of inciting more nightmares. But, as the tears came from writing the second piece, so did the reminder that the shame is only valid if I hold onto it. Writing it in letter format, especially to my heart, made me feel as though I was finally comforting myself, giving myself permission to break down, to not be strong. Healing takes work... But is worth it.
Tiffini Johnson

Composing this letter became an act of reclamation for me and a statement of hope for others. It was a reminder that we need not sacrifice ours gifts to trauma and abuse; they are in us and with us, and if we are paying attention they will call us back from the abyss of abuse. It takes courage to surrender to the healing and it is worth every word.
Marylyn L. Tesconi

Portable Homes became a space of love and grace for me. For this I will be eternally grateful. Originally, I was sent information from a relative who was more familiar with the scope of the project. Both of us had experienced difficult and traumatic life events, and she wanted to share with me how much participation in this project had helped her. She relayed the healing that she experienced by writing about her stories. I was cautious at first, afraid to take that first step forward, uncertain as to what the outcome would be. I needn't have worried. The loving and confidential space that was provided by Lexie Bean, made the project simply amazing. Release, safety, a sense of normalcy returning, these are just some of the emotions that were evoked in me as I crafted my pieces. At the end of the day, we must all recognize, that the way the world is healed, the way we all hold hands and heal in a space of loving acceptance, is one step, one passage, one project, one heart, at a time.
Colleen Fusetti

Share something!

If you would like to make a love letter, treaty, oath, prayer, manifesto, or a poem to a body part, please see the guidelines below to join the movement. All bodies and forms are welcome!

- Your piece may take on the form of a written letter, visual art, or video / audio recording
- Your piece should focus on one body part. Feel free to explore its relationship to other body parts and/or your body as a whole, or even its relationship to others' bodies.
- Remember it's a letter to yourself, not about yourself.
- Write and make in the language or combination of languages that feel closest to your body and experiences in it.
- Feel free to make more than one!

Send all pieces to attnpeoplewithbodyparts@gmail.com. (please include your name, preferred pronouns, and city.) You may also contact this email address if the process puts you in a dark place or if you would like general writing moral support.

For additional support, please visit the Resources section of our website and people and places that feel safe for you.

About this guy

LEXIE BEAN, A RECENT GRADUATE FROM OBERLIN COLLEGE, IS A BODY-POSITIVE ACTIVIST THAT PLAYS WITH DANCE, WRITING, AND COLLABORATIVE ARTS PROJECTS. SHE WOULD PROBABLY LIKE TO GO ROLLER SKATING WITH YOU. THIS IS HER SECOND ANTHOLOGY PUBLISHED UNDER THE MOVING MOVEMENT ATTENTION: PEOPLE WITH BODY PARTS.

www.attnpeoplewithbodyparts.org

And friends

SHELBY ZIESING, A DREAMER AND ASPIRING EDUCATOR. SHE LIKES TO MAKE THINGS.

STEVEN JAMES PLOE, HE LIKES BASEBALL AND MAKES CAMPY HORROR MOVIES SOMETIMES. HE'S THE ONLY KNOWN HUMAN TO KNOW THE MEANING OF "ZIGAZIG AH."

THOMAS ANYEL IRVING, A VISUAL ARTS STUDENT ATTENDING COLLEGE FOR CREATIVE STUDIES IN DETROIT. HE IS WRITING A BIO. HE IS SERVING THE FOOD. HE KNOWS ABOUT YOUR PARTY. HE IS CALLING YOU "DUDE!"

TAILS WILLIAMS, A CAT MOM. SHE ASPIRES TO BECOME ONE WITH THE SPAGHETTI NIRVANA. AND MAYBE A PROFESSIONAL ARTIST.

LAURA GROTHAUS, A WRITER AND ARTIST FROM CINCINNATI, OHIO. SHE LIKES MOVING AND BEING MOVED.